THE
INDOOR
PLANT
BIBLE

THE INDOOR PLANT BIBLE

The essential guide to choosing and caring for indoor, greenhouse, and patio plants

DORTE NISSEN

A QUARTO BOOK

First edition for North America published in 2005 by Barron's Educational Series, Inc.

All inquiries should be addressed to:
Barron's Educational Series, Inc.
250 Wireless Boulevard
Hauppauge, NY 11788
http://www.barronseduc.com

International Standard Book Number
0-7641-5769-8
Library of Congress Catalog Card Number
2003113352

QUAR.HPB

Conceived, designed, and produced by
Quarto Publishing plc
The Old Brewery
6 Blundell Street
London N7 9BH

Project editor Jo Fisher
Art editor Anna Knight
Designer Helen Garvey
Assistant art director Penny Cobb
Copy editor Fiona Robertson
Photographer Mark Winwood
Illustrator Michelle Stamp
Picture researcher Claudia Tate
Proofreader Louise Armstrong
Indexer Geraldine Beare

Art director Moira Clinch
Publisher Piers Spence

Color separation by Modern Age,
Hong Kong
Printed by Midas Printing International Ltd,
China

9 8 7 6 5 4 3 2 1

Contents

How to use this book

This book is laid out to give the maximum amount of information in the clearest possible way. An introductory section on plant care contains general advice on keeping your plants healthy and looking their best. This includes tips on watering, a description of how to pot a plant, and the easiest methods of propagation.

The main part of the book is the plant directory. Arranged alphabetically by botanical name, it lists 140 of the most popular and exciting indoor plants. Each plant is examined individually in a succinct, easy-to-read format.

A glossary on page 252 explains any unfamiliar botanical terms.

Plant care symbols summarizing the ideal growth conditions. See key to symbols opposite; in addition, a handy pull-out version is included at the back of this book that can be used while flicking through the directory.

Family name

Common names

Botanical name

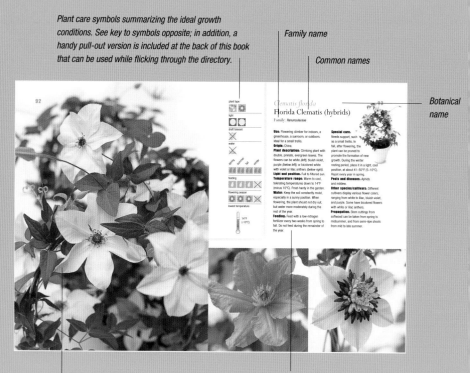

Picture of healthy plant showing color and shape.

Plant information: This ranges from a description of the plant and its origin, through to optimum conditions for growth in terms of light, temperature, and feeding. Any special care issues are discussed, along with a description of other relevant cultivars and methods of propagation. Temperatures are given in both Imperial and metric forms and, for ease of use, units have been rounded to the nearest convenient figure.

Key to symbols

Plant type

Foliage plant

Flowering plant

Climbing or trailing plant

Fruiting plant

Large plant

Light

Plant prefers full sun

Plant prefers indirect light

Plant prefers shade

Draft tolerance

Tolerates drafts

Will not tolerate drafts

Watering

Plant requires misting

Plant requires steeping

Water plant in its urn-like rosette

No special watering requirements

The symbols below are arranged by season

Water regularly

Water less frequently

Do not water

Feeding

Feed regularly

Do not feed

Flowering season

In flower

No flowers

Lowest temperature

50°F
(-10°C)

Indicates the lowest temperature at which the plant will survive

Section 1

Plant care

Choosing the right houseplants and keeping them healthy need not be difficult. This section offers some general guidance on selecting the right plant for your environment and looks at different methods of watering and feeding. Potting, pruning, and propagation techniques are described and a "plant clinic" is included, giving some solutions to common houseplant problems.

Choosing indoor plants

Choosing indoor plants requires some thought. Consider which plants suit your personal taste, the interior style of your home, and the space available. Think about how much time you can spend on plant care every day. If you're a busy person with little spare time, don't buy plants that need daily watering. If you want your plants to last for a long time you must select the right plant for your home environment. Use the checklist below to help you find the most suitable plants and make sure that any plants you buy are top quality. Be critical when you choose where to buy your plants. If a plant has been neglected before being sold to you, its life may be shortened. The plant must look healthy, with unbroken leaves of the right color, without scorch marks or brown tips or edges. Flowering plants should have many healthy buds that are yet to open; otherwise, flowering may last for only a short time. The plant should also have a pleasing overall shape.

Epipremnum pinnatum

CHECKLIST

- Is the plant labeled? The label should tell you the plant's name and how to take care of it.
- Has the potting mixture dried out? If so, the plant has been neglected—do not buy it.
- How much light does the plant need? You may need to keep it in direct sunlight.
- How much water does the plant need? It may require watering every day during summer.
- How long will the plant survive without being watered?

- What temperature does the plant require? It may not survive at normal room temperature.
- Is the plant poisonous? This is an important consideration if small children will be in the house.
- Does the plant require special care?
- Is the plant easy or difficult to grow?
- Look at both sides of the leaves. Can you see any sign of pests or diseases?

◀ **Transporting plants**

After choosing and buying your plants, have them wrapped in protective sleeves. This will protect them both from cold and strong sunlight, and also guard against knocks. Do not leave plants in a cold or hot car because very high or low temperatures might harm them.

Euphorbia milii

Temperature

Plants growing outside will often be exposed to a broad range of temperatures. In modern houses, however, heating systems ensure a fairly consistent temperature of about 68–73°F (20–23°C). Although tropical and subtropical plants like to be kept at about 64–70°F (18–20°C), many plants from subtropical areas prefer a dormant period during winter, at a lower temperature. Most plants from temperate areas prefer lower temperatures than those found indoors, and tolerate frost during winter. If kept indoors during winter, their flowers will last for a shorter period than if they had been placed at a lower temperature outside.

Indoor temperatures can be variable, so keep this in mind when choosing a plant's location. Rooms such as bedrooms or guest rooms, for example, are often cooler. Avoid placing plants close to radiators, where temperatures will be high and the air very dry. Strong sunlight through south-facing windows will result in high temperatures, and may scorch some plants. Open doors or windows allow cool air to rush in and cause temperatures to drop sharply, which may not be tolerated by some indoor plants.

Many plants have a broad tolerance to temperature, but it is important that they should be allowed to acclimatize slowly to higher or lower temperatures. Temperature preferences will be indicated under the description of each plant.

Dormant period

Many indoor plants need a resting period during winter. If this is the case, the preferred temperature will be recommended in the plant description. Plants from temperate areas, which prefer cool temperatures, are often frost-hardy in the garden during winter. It's important to remember that these plants should be planted out in the garden no later than August to ensure that a root system becomes well established before winter and that they acclimatize slowly to the lower temperatures.

77°F (25°C)
Warm
A plant that prefers a warm location enjoys temperatures above 64°F (18°C).

68°F (20°C)
Warm to cool
A plant that prefers a warm to cool location tolerates temperatures from 68°F (25°C) down to 59°F (15°C), or even cooler.

50°F (10°C)
Cool
A plant that prefers a cool location enjoys temperatures below 59°F (15°C).

Light conditions

Light is essential to plants, but the exact amount required depends on the growing conditions of the plant in its natural environment. Plants like cactuses and succulents, for example, often grow in desert areas and are exposed to strong, direct sunlight, while plants growing at the bottom of the rainforest, like *Peperomia*, receive very little light.

A plant is affected by both the intensity and the duration of light. Most plants from tropical or subtropical areas need twelve to sixteen hours of light per day to grow. This makes growth difficult during northern winters, when there are only seven to eight hours of daylight, and light intensity is also low. It is a good idea therefore to place such plants close to the window during winter or to use artificial light. Many plants from subtropical areas, where the winters are cold, prefer a dormant period during this time. If cared for indoors, allow these plants a winter rest period, when they should be kept dry in a light and cool location.

Long-day, short-day, and day-neutral plants

In general, flowering plants need more light than foliage plants if they are to produce flower buds. However, flower-bud formation can also be based on day length. Long-day plants will only flower if they have received more than twelve hours of light per day during a certain period. Flower formation in short-day plants is promoted by less than twelve hours of light per day during the required period. The third group of plants are day-neutral, which means that they do not depend on a certain amount of light each day to make them flower. Flower formation can also be promoted by a cool period, letting the soil dry out, or letting the plant reach a certain age. In this book a light preference, which may be "direct sun" (direct light), "filtered sun" (indirect light), or "shady position" (full shade) is indicated in the description of each plant.

Direct sun (direct light)

Plants requiring direct sun should be exposed to direct sun for most of the day, in a south-facing window for example. Plants in an east- or north-facing window will also receive direct sun, but for

fewer hours. Direct sun is found up to 3⅓ ft. (1 m) from the window. Sometimes sunlight will cause parts of a plant to redden—the leaves of *Kalanchoe blossfeldiana*, for instance—but this red coloring is harmless to the plant. A broad range of indoor plants can be placed in west- and east-facing windows, but only a few will tolerate the direct sun of a south-facing window at midday during summer.

Filtered sun (indirect light)

Filtered sun is found between 3⅓ ft. (1 m) and 5¼ ft. (1.5 m) from a window receiving sun all day or during part of the day. Filtered sun is also found up to 3⅓ ft. (1 m) from a window if the sun is filtered through a translucent curtain or a tree. Most plants prefer this position.

Shady position (full shade)

Shade is found in an area 5¼–6⅔ ft. (1.5–2 m) from a sunny window. It is also the light of a north-facing window. This amount of light is only a quarter of the light found in direct sun.

Poor light

Poor light is found in areas more than 6⅔ ft. (2 m) away from a window receiving sun all day or during most of the day. The light intensity will be so poor that no plant will thrive, even if the area seems well lit to the human eye. If you want to place plants here, you will need to provide a source of artificial light.

Artificial light

Light bulbs or tubes suitable for promoting plant growth can be bought in gardening stores or at aquarium suppliers. To have the optimum effect, place the light source ⅓–⅔ ft. (30–50 cm) from the plant. If kept in an area of poor light, make sure that foliage plants receive twelve to sixteen hours of artificial light per day, and flowering plants sixteen to eighteen hours.

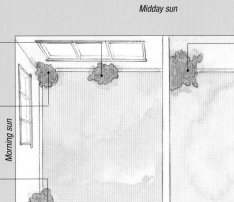

This large window will get plenty of sun all day.

Plants needing moderate conditions but good light are well placed here.

Many types of foliage plants will live happily here, provided the corner is not too dark.

Midday sun

Morning sun

Evening sun

Ferns may appreciate the shade if humidity and temperature are suitable.

A shady room has a low light level most of the day.

The light is obstructed by a tree, but there will be warm evening light on most days.

Watering

Water is essential to all plants; they will die without it. Some plants need to be watered often; other plants, especially succulents and cacti, can survive for up to a few months without being watered, and will die if overwatered.

Suitable water for plants

All plants must be watered with lukewarm water, which means water at room temperature. Cold water may damage a plant's roots, leaves, or flowers. In general, the water should be as lime-free as possible. Tap water may be used, but it often has a high lime content that will damage some plants. These plants must be watered with soft water, such as rainwater or cooled boiled water.

How to water

Specific instructions about watering are given in the description of each plant. You should water until liquid begins to flow through the drainage holes at the bottom of the container. Throw away the water in the saucer after five minutes, as most plants do not tolerate standing in water. However, some plants tolerate or even prefer standing in water. This mainly applies to marsh plants, which must be kept constantly moist.

It is important to use the right amount of water because plants will be damaged by too much or too little. Houseplants often die because of overwatering.

▲ Clean large-leaved foliage plants and give them a natural shine by lightly wiping with a little warmed milk.

Keep the soil constantly moist and avoid drying out

Some plants are sensitive to drying out, which may cause leaves or flowers to drop. Water these plants often and plentifully, which in summer may mean every day. Keep the potting mixture constantly moist and do not allow the surface of the soil to dry out.

▶ When liquid flows from the drainage holes in the bottom of the container, the plant has been watered sufficiently.

▲ Water regularly, allowing the soil to dry out before watering again

Water most indoor plants moderately. Water so that the potting mixture is moist all the way through, and allow the surface of the soil to dry out to a depth of ⅓–1 in. (1–3 cm) before watering again.

Water sparingly

Some plants need only a little water. Water so that the potting mixture is barely moist throughout, and allow ⅓–1 in. (1–3 cm) of the mixture to dry out before watering again.

Keep the soil almost dry during winter

Hardy plants should be kept cool for a dormant period in winter. Keep the potting mixture barely moist, and allow it to dry out before watering again.

Special watering

Some plants require special care during watering. For instance, they may need to be watered from underneath, rather than directly onto the soil, to avoid standing water around the bulb and roots.

▲ Water in the urn-like rosette

The leaves of the *Bromeliaceae* family often form an urn-like rosette. Water these plants inside the rosette, which must always contain water if the plant is kept in a warm position.

▶ Mist frequently with a hand-spray

Some plants are able to absorb mist through their leaves and some plants prefer high humidity.

◀ Water from underneath

Add water to the saucer, leaving ⅓ in. (1 cm) in the saucer for five minutes. Add more water if necessary, then throw away the surplus water after a further five minutes.

Feeding

To grow, plants need light, water, and minerals. Potted plants are normally sold in a potting mixture with added nutrients. These nutrients will last for about six weeks (read the instructions on the label; the length of time will vary depending on the type of potting mixture used). After this period you should start fertilizing the plant yourself.

As a general rule, fertilize only when the plant is in active growth, which is mainly from spring through summer. It is not necessary to feed the plant during the remainder of the year. Overfeeding can do as much damage as underfeeding, so feed no more than the amount recommended in this book or on the fertilizer label. Give fast-growing plants more food than slow-growing ones.

▲ Plant fed with a slow-release fertilizer spike.

Standard low-nitrogen fertilizer

Feed most indoor plants with a low-nitrogen liquid fertilizer, which should be added to the water you use for watering. Plants with a high nutrient requirement are best fed every two weeks from spring to fall; those with a lower nutrient requirement, once a month from spring to fall. Feed plants with a very low nutrient requirement with a weak fertilizer, that is, half the concentration of a standard fertilizer.

Orchid fertilizer

Orchids require slightly different nutrients from other indoor plants; use a special orchid fertilizer.

Acid fertilizer

Lime-intolerant plants require an acid fertilizer.

Slow-release fertilizer

Slow-release fertilizers come in the form of spikes or pills. Push spikes in at the edge of the potting mixture and water them well to dissolve the fertilizer. Add pills to the mixture during potting or push them in later with a pencil (avoid damaging the roots).

Foliar fertilizer spray

Plants that absorb water through the leaves, such as bromeliads, will benefit from a foliar fertilizer spray. Dilute to the correct concentration and spray over both sides of the leaves.

Pruning, Deadheading, and Cutting Back

Indoor plants need to be pruned now and then so that they retain an attractive, balanced appearance. Flowering plants also require deadheading—cutting dead or faded flowers from the main stem with a pair of scissors. Deadhead plants like cyclamens by twisting and pulling out the whole flower stalk from the base.

Cutting back encourages healthy new growth by removing the old, weak parts of a plant. It also ensures that your favorite plants do not grow too large for the house. Cut back the plant in fall or early spring, before active new growth begins. Whether you use a craft knife or a pair of scissors or shears, it is important that your tool is sharp and clean.

Always cut above the bud, where new shoots form, and cut downward, away from the bud.

▲ Tall plants

Cut tall plants back drastically by cutting off the top of the woody stem. After cutting back, place the plant in optimum growing conditions to promote the formation of new shoots and leaves.

▶ Climbing plants

Cut straggly growth back from climbing plants after unwinding stems from the hoop or trellis. Cut off shoots until only a few of the youngest stems remain, then wind these stems around the support again.

◀ Long-stemmed plants

Pinch out the growing tips of plants that naturally form long stems to secure a more compact growth. Cut or nip out growing tips with your fingers.

▶ Trailing plants

Cut back stems that have large gaps between the leaves to promote dense new growth. Cut the stem back to the node where tight growth is seen. New growth will be more compact if the plant is allowed more light after cutting back.

Potting and repotting

Almost any container can be used for potted plants, but the size of the pot must fit the size of the plant. Pots with drainage holes that allow excess water to seep away provide the best conditions for healthy growth. If you use pots without holes, line them with drainage material and be more careful not to overwater the plant.

Repotting

In general, fast-growing foliage plants and flowering plants like to be repotted once a year. Larger foliage plants and slow-growing cactuses and succulents only need to be repotted every second or third year. Repot orchids when their container is full of roots. In general, repot potted plants before new growth starts, mainly in early spring. Information about the timing and frequency of repotting is given under the description of each plant. A plant may also need repotting at other times of the year. If the potting mixture dries out quickly after watering, the plant has probably outgrown its container. Check whether the roots have sufficient space by removing the plant from its container, as follows:

1 ▲ Water the plant well, then leave it for an hour.

2 ▼ Turn the pot upside down and gently tap its edge on the side of a table.

3 ◄ Let the plant and its root ball slide out.

4 Check whether the roots have enough space. If the roots fill the whole pot, the plant should be repotted.

How to repot a plant

If repotting is required, follow the procedure for removing the plant from its container as described opposite. Then:

1 ◀ Put a small amount of potting mixture in a larger, clean pot.

2 ▶ Place the root ball above the potting mixture at the desired height. Adjust the amount of potting mixture in the base of the container.

Types of potting mixture

Do not use soil from the garden. It may not be suitable for indoor plants, and may be contaminated with pests and diseases. Various types of potting mixture are available:

Ready-mix potting mixture

A ready-mix will usually provide the best conditions for healthy growth. Standard potting mixture, which is mainly peat-based, is sterilized and therefore free from pests and diseases. Slow-release nutrients are usually added by the producer.

Special potting mixtures

Certain plants need special treatment. Orchids have unique requirements, so it's recommended to pot them in orchid mixture. Some plants, such as rhododendrons, prefer a more acid potting mixture. Potting mixture free of fertilizer must be used for propagating cuttings and seeds.

3 ▶ Fill in around the edges with potting mixture, and press down firmly with your fingers..

4 Leave a gap of ½–1 in. (1–2.5 cm) between the surface of the soil and the rim of the pot for watering.

5 ▼ Water the plant thoroughly.

Propagation

Some indoor plants are easy to propagate; others are more difficult. Each plant entry tells you about the easiest way to propagate the plant and the best time of the year to do so. The most common methods of propagation are described here:

◄ Seeds

A few indoor plants produce seeds that can be harvested, but a broad range of seeds can be bought. The best time for sowing seeds is in spring.

▲ Plantlets or offsets

Cut plantlets off the parent plant and plant them in a separate pot. Gently break off from the main stem well-developed offsets with some roots and pot. Plantlets and offsets can be taken at any time of the year.

Leaf cuttings

1 ► Cut healthy, mature leaves from the parent plant close to the end of the leaf stalk.

2 ▼ Some gardeners recommend dipping the end of the leaf stalk in rooting hormone powder.

3 ▼ Insert the cutting into some rooting mixture so that the base of the leaf itself touches the surface.

Stem cuttings

Take softwood cuttings from nonflowering shoots in early spring, before new growth begins. Greenwood cuttings are similar to softwood cuttings but take the cuttings later, when the new growth is beginning to firm up. Semi-ripe cuttings have a hard base and a soft tip. Take these in summer or early fall; they should be 2–4 in. (5–10 cm) long. Hardwood cuttings have both hard bases and tips and should be about 8 in. (20 cm) long. Take these cuttings from fall to early winter, when the current season's growth has matured.

1 ◀ Cut off a 1¾–2 in. (4–5 cm) piece of stem with two to three pairs of leaves.

2 ▶ Remove the lowest pair of leaves and the soft tip from the shoot just above the node.

3 ◀ Dip the end of the stem in rooting powder if desired. Place the cutting into some rooting mixture.

Plant division

Most plants forming a clump can be propagated by dividing the clump. After watering well, take the plant out of its pot and gently separate it by pulling away single sections or clusters. If the sections are joined with thickened roots, a knife may be needed to separate them.

Rooting mixture

For all propagation methods, always use a suitable peat-based, nutrient-free rooting mixture. When the roots have formed and the new plants are large enough, pot the plants in a standard or special potting mixture, depending on the plant species.

Propagators

Some tropical plant cuttings need a source of bottom heat to promote the formation of roots. This may be supplied by using a heated propagator or a propagation blanket. The temperature should be 68–77°F (20–25°C).

Plant Doctor

Leaf clinic

Symptom	Possible cause	Cure
Leaves lack their usual color and look dull.	Too much/insufficient light. Spider mites and/or mealy bugs. Undernourishment. Dirt on the leaves.	Move the plant to a shadier or lighter position. Fight spider mites and/or mealy bugs with insect soap and/or a biological control. Check the feeding requirements; fertilize if necessary. Give the plant a shower.
Yellowing of upper leaves.	A lime-intolerant plant.	Repot in a more acid potting mixture, and always use rainwater or cooled boiled water when watering.
Mottled patches on leaves.	Scorching during watering. Plant disease.	Water the plant from underneath. Treat disease *(see below)*. Throw away the plant if the stems become stunted and/or deformed.
Lower leaves dry up and drop off.	Temperature too high. Insufficient light. Underwatering.	Check the plant's location and move it if necessary. Give the plant more water.
Variegated leaves become completely green.	Insufficient light.	Move plant to a lighter location.
Lower leaves turn yellow and drop off.	This could be completely natural—all plants lose some leaves sometimes. Overwatering.	Check the moisture content of the potting mixture. If it's saturated, always let the soil dry out before watering again.
Leaves curl up and drop off.	Underwatering. Temperature too cool/exposure to cold draughts.	Check the moisture content of the potting mixture. If it's dry, increase the amount of water provided regularly. If the pot has expanded away from the soil, submerge it in a bucket of water until the potting mixture is saturated. Check the location recommended for the plant.
Wilting leaves.	Under- or overwatering. Plant may be pot-bound.	Check the plant's watering requirements and act accordingly. You may need to move the plant to a cooler location. Check if the plant's roots fill the whole pot. If so, repot *(see Potting and repotting, page 20)*.
Sudden leaf drop.	A recent change of environment. (Has the plant just been moved from the garden center to your home, for example?)	Give all plants special care, keeping them out of direct sun, during the first few days in a new environment. Check if the plant needs repotting.
Brown leaf tips or edges.	Plant may be pot-bound. Lack of humidity. Scorching during watering.	Mist the plant frequently with soft water. Do not water the plant when it is in direct sunlight.

Flower clinic

Symptom	Possible cause	Cure
Flowers fade quickly.	Temperature too high. Underwatering. Lack of humidity. Insufficient light. A lime-intolerant plant.	Check the temperature requirements and adjust accordingly. Is the potting mixture too dry? If so, increase the amount of water provided regularly. Increase humidity by misting daily with soft water. Move the plant into a lighter location.
Plants fails to flower.	Too little light. Dormant period required. Overfeeding. Plant may be pot-bound.	This may be a short- or long-day plant, which requires a certain amount of light to flower. It may need a dormant period to produce flower buds. Check all the conditions required to promote flower formation in this plant. Check if the plant needs repotting.

Plant clinic

Symptom	Possible cause	Cure
White coating on leaves and stems.	Powdery mildew.	Keep the plant isolated from other plants. Cut away the affected part and place the plant in optimal growing conditions. Avoid wetting the leaves. Alternatively, discard the plant.
Slow growth.	Insufficient fertilizer. Plant may be pot-bound. Overwatering. Pest infestation.	It may be that your plant is simply in its dormant period. If not, make sure that you feed the plant regularly. Check whether repotting is needed. Reduce watering if it does not match the plant's requirements. Examine the whole plant for pests. Treat with insect soap or a biological control if it has been attacked.
Small leaves and spindly growth.	Insufficient fertilizer. Spider mites.	Feed the plant regularly if it is in active growth. Check under the leaves for spider mites. If you find any, cut away the affected parts and spray with insect soap and/or use a biological control.
Plants are sticky and/or mottled with a black substance.	Sooty mold and/or aphids and/or white fly.	Sooty mold grows on honeydew, which is the excreta of aphids, white fly, mealy bugs, and scale insects. Check for white fly infestation by shaking the plant. Pick out aphids with your fingers and suck up white fly with a vacuum cleaner. Spray the infected parts with insect soap and/or use a biological control.
Fluffy gray mold on any part of the plant.	Gray mold.	Gray mold is a fungus that thrives in cool, damp conditions. It may infect soft-leaved plants, especially if the plant is overwatered. Cut off all affected parts and scrape away any infected potting mixture. Keep the plant drier and in optimal growing conditions, but isolated from other plants. Discard the plant if it is badly infected.

Section 2

Directory of plants

Arranged alphabetically by botanical name, this section of the book lists 140 of the most popular houseplants. Each entry contains a description of the plant and instructions for its care, including its preferences in terms of light, temperature, watering, and feeding. Any pests and diseases known to attack the plant are listed and the best methods of propagation outlined.

Abutilon
Flowering Maple/Indian Mallow/Parlor Maple (hybrids)

Family: *Malvaceae*

Use: Flowering shrub for indoors, a greenhouse or sunroom, or outdoors.

Origin: Brazil.

Plant description: Flowering shrub displaying large, heart-shaped, grass-green leaves with yellow or white blotches. The decorative pendant, bell-shaped flowers can be white, yellow, orange, purple, pink, salmon, or dark red. A nectar-producing plant.

Light and position: Filtered sunlight. Place the plant in full sun only during winter.

Temperature range: Warm, cooler during winter. Tolerates temperatures down to 41°F (5°C).

Water: Water plentifully from spring to fall, and sparingly in winter. Do not let the plant dry out when flowering, or the flower buds will drop.

Feeding: Feed with a low-nitrogen fertilizer once a week from spring to fall. Do not feed during the remainder of the year.

Special care: This plant needs support. It prefers a dormant period during winter, when it should be kept in a light, cool position at about 41–50°F (5–10°C). Repot every year in early spring. At the same time, cut back long shoots to promote bushy new growth.

Pests and diseases: Aphids, spider mites, and white fly. A sudden change in temperature may result in yellow leaves and leaf drop.

Other species/cultivars: *A. megapotamicum* is a smaller, bushy shrub with slender, drooping branches; ideal for hanging baskets or training to a hoop. The leaves are heart- or arrow-shaped, often with green or yellow blotches. The flowers are smaller and pendulous, and their colorful, inflated calyces cause them to resemble lanterns.

Propagation: Stem cuttings can be taken from softwood or greenwood at any time of year.

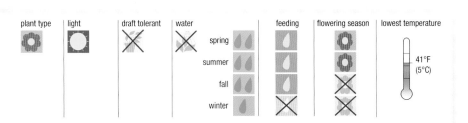

plant type	light	draft tolerant	water		feeding	flowering season	lowest temperature
			spring				
			summer				41°F (5°C)
			fall				
			winter				

plant type

light

draft tolerant

water

spring summer fall winter

feeding

flowering season

⊠ ⊠ ⊠ ⊠

lowest temperature

50°F
(10°C)

Acalypha wilkesiana
Copperleaf/Jacob's Coat/Beefsteak Plant/
Firedragon/Match-Me-If-You-Can

Family: *Euphorbiaceae*

Use: Foliage plant for indoors, or a greenhouse or sunroom in summer.
Origin: Pacific Islands.
Plant description: Branching shrub cultivated for its striking oval leaves in bright shades of red, copper, metallic green, or yellow-green. Small flowers are found in spikes at the top of the plant, but have no ornamental value.
Light and position: Full sun to filtered sun. The colors of the leaves will be brighter if the plant is exposed to direct sunlight.

Temperature range: Warm to cool, tolerating temperatures down to 50°F (10°C).
Water: Keep the soil moist, especially during summer. Avoid letting the soil dry out.
Feeding: Feed with a low-nitrogen fertilizer every two weeks from spring to fall. Do not feed during the remainder of the year.
Special care: Repot every year in spring. At the same time, cut back long shoots to promote bushy new growth.
Pests and diseases: Spider mites.
Other species/cultivars: There are many cultivars, offering a variety of leaf colors.
Propagation: Cuttings with three leaves can be taken from the top of the stem in spring.

Desert Rose/Desert Azalea/Mock Azalea/
Impala Lily/Kudu Lily/Sabi Star
Family: *Apocynaceae*

Use: Sculptural foliage and flowering succulent for indoors, a greenhouse, or a sunroom.

Origin: Egypt, Sudan, Ethiopia, East Africa, and Arabia.

Plant description: Succulent shrub that forms a thick caudex, with a mass of short branches tipped with glossy, dark green leaves. The funnel-shaped flowers are carmine, pink, or white with a yellow center.

Light and position: Prefers full sunlight; tolerates filtered sun.

Temperature range: Warm, cooler during winter. Tolerates temperatures down to 50°F (10°C).

Water: This plant will rot and die if overwatered. Water regularly but sparingly from spring to fall. Keep the soil almost dry from October to April.

Feeding: Feed with a low-nitrogen fertilizer once a month from spring to fall. Do not feed during the remainder of the year.

Special care: The plant produces a milky sap that can cause irritation; avoid contact with skin or eyes. This shrub needs a dormant period from October to April, when it should be kept in a light, cool position, at about 59°F (15°C). Repot every second or third year in spring.

Pests and diseases: Gray mold, basal rots if overwatered.

Other species/cultivars: Four other Adenium species are found, but rarely cultivated.

Propagation: From seeds in spring or stem cuttings in summer.

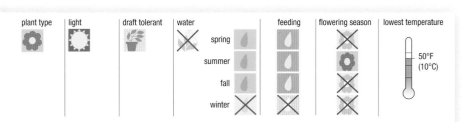

plant type	light	draft tolerant	water		feeding	flowering season	lowest temperature
			spring				
			summer				50°F (10°C)
			fall				
			winter				

Adiantum raddianum
Delta Maidenhair Fern

Family: *Pteridaceae*

Use: Ornamental fern for indoors, or a greenhouse or sunroom in summer.

Origin: Central America and tropical South America.

Plant description: Delicate in appearance, this fern has leaves that are first erect and later curving, with many small, light green leaflets. The basal leafstalks are shiny black.

Light and position: Filtered sunlight to shade; avoid direct sunlight.

Temperature range: Warm to cool, tolerating temperatures down to 41°F (5°C).

Water: Water regularly with soft water in growing season, allowing the soil to dry out slightly before watering again. Water more sparingly during the rest of the year. Mist frequently with a hand-spray to maintain high humidity.

Feeding: Feed with a low-nitrogen fertilizer once a month from spring to fall. Do not feed during the remainder of the year.

Special care: This plant prefers high humidity and can be difficult to keep for a long time. Repot every year in spring.

Pests and diseases: Gray mold, aphids, scale insects, and mealy bugs.

Other species/cultivars: Cultivars include 'Fritz-Luthi,' with dense leaves; 'Lisa,' a very compact plant; and 'Bronze Venus,' with bronze-colored young leaves.

Propagation: By division of rhizomes in early spring or from fresh spores.

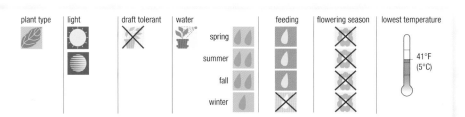

plant type	light	draft tolerant	water		feeding	flowering season	lowest temperature
				spring			
				summer			41°F (5°C)
				fall			
				winter			

Aechmea fasciata
Urn Plant/ Vase Plant

Family: *Bromeliaceae*

Use: Flowering bromeliad for indoors, or a greenhouse or sunroom in summer.

Origin: Brazil.

Plant description: An epiphytic, tender perennial forming a rosette of leathery, green leaves covered with gray scales and banded silvery gray, with a delightful vase-like appearance. The inflorescence is durable and very striking, with spiky pink bracts and blue flowers.

Light and position: The plant tolerates a broad spectrum of light, but keep it away from full sunlight.

Temperature range: Warm to cool temperatures, down to 46°F (8°C).

Water: Use lukewarm water. The plant tolerates drying out for a few weeks.

Feeding: Feed with a low-nitrogen fertilizer inside the rosette once a month from spring to fall. Do not feed during the remainder of the year.

Special care: Water and fertilize inside the urn-like rosette, which should always contain water except when the plant is kept at a low temperature. Repot offsets in early spring.

Pests and diseases: Mealy bugs.

Other species/cultivars: None.

Propagation: After flowering, the inflorescence dies but offsets are formed in the leaf axils. Divide the plant in early summer, when the offsets have grown to half the size of the parent plant.

plant type	light	draft tolerant	water		feeding	flowering season	lowest temperature
			spring				
			summer				46°F (8°C)
			fall				
			winter				

Aeschynanthus
Basket Plant/Lipstick Vine/
Blush Wort (hybrids)

Family: *Gesneriaceae*

Use: Flowering trailer for indoors, or a greenhouse or sunroom in summer; ideal for hanging baskets.

Plant description: Epiphytic trailer with succulent, lance-shaped leaves, dark green in color. The curving, tubular flowers are flaming orange, crimson-red, or black-purple, with protruding white style.

Light and position: Filtered sunlight to shade. Keep the plant away from full sun.

Temperature range: Warm, cooler during winter. Tolerates temperatures down to 50°F (10°C).

Water: Water regularly with soft water from spring to fall, more sparingly during winter. The plant will tolerate a slight drying out. Avoid letting water stand on the leaves.

Feeding: Use a low-nitrogen fertilizer once a month from spring to fall. Do not feed during the remainder of the year.

Special care: The plant needs a rest period in winter, when it should be kept in a light and cool position, at about 54°F (12°C). Water sparingly during this time to promote flowering. Repot every year in spring.

Pests and diseases: Aphids and spider mites.

Other species/cultivars: The cultivar 'Caroline' has smaller leaves; 'Mona Lisa' has larger leaves; 'Rubens' is an erect shrub with flaming orange flowers. The species *A. marmoratus* is a foliage trailer with dark green leaves blotched with maroon.

Propagation: In early spring, from stem cuttings or tip cuttings with one pair of leaves.

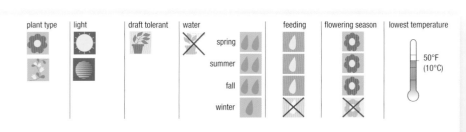

plant type	light	draft tolerant	water		feeding	flowering season	lowest temperature
				spring			
				summer			50°F (10°C)
				fall			
				winter			

Agave americana
Century Plant/American Aloe

Family: *Agavaceae*

Use: Sculptural succulent for indoors, or a greenhouse or sunroom in summer.

Origin: Mexico.

Plant description: A stemless rosette of broad, thick, and succulent gray-green leaves with spiky tips and sharp brown spines at the margins.

Light and position: Prefers full sunlight; tolerates filtered sun.

Temperature range: Warm to cool, cooler during winter. Tolerates temperatures down to 32°F (0°C).

Water: This plant will die if overwatered. Water regularly but sparingly from spring to fall, keeping the soil almost dry in winter.

Feeding: Feed with a low-nitrogen fertilizer once a month from spring to fall. Do not feed during the rest of the year.

Special care: The plant needs a dormant period from October to April, when it should be kept in a light, cool position, at about 41°F (5°C). Repot every second or third year in early spring.

Pests and diseases: None.

Other species/cultivars: The cultivar 'Variegata' has yellow-edged leaves. About 100 species of *Agave* are found, some of which are cultivated. *A. stricta* has linear leaves, colored gray with dark green. *A. parryi* has gray leaves with brown to gray terminal spines. *A. victoriae-reginae* has keeled, dark green leaves with white margins.

Propagation: Separate the young plants during spring and summer. They can be planted in clumps or as single rosettes.

plant type

light

draft tolerant

water

spring   summer   fall   winter

feeding

flowering season

lowest temperature

32°F
(0°C)

Aglaonema commutatum

Philippine Evergreen/
Aglaonema Aroid

Family: *Araceae*

Use: Tough foliage plant for indoors.
Origin: The Philippines.
Plant description: Herbaceous plant with elliptic leaves, colored deep green with markings of yellow- or silver-gray.
Light and position: Tolerates a shady position to filtered sun. Keep away from direct sunlight.
Temperature range: Warm to cool temperatures, down to 59°F (15°C).
Water: Water regularly in growing season, allowing the soil to dry out slightly before watering again, and more sparingly during the rest of the year. The plant prefers high humidity and should be misted frequently with a hand-spray.
Feeding: Feed with a low-nitrogen fertilizer every two weeks from spring to fall. Do not feed during the remainder of the year.
Special care: Repot every year in spring.
Pests and diseases: Aphids, scale insects, spider mites, and mealy bugs.
Other species/cultivars: The cultivar 'Maria Christina' has large leaves with yellow-green markings. 'Pattaya Beauty' has larger leaves marked with dark green and olive-green. The leaves of 'Silver Queen' are almost entirely silver-green.
Propagation: Divide the plant in spring.

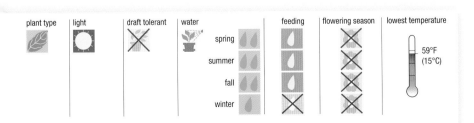

plant type	light	draft tolerant	water		feeding	flowering season	lowest temperature
			spring				59°F (15°C)
			summer				
			fall				
			winter				

Allamanda cathartica

Golden Trumpet/Allamanda

Family: *Apocynaceae*

Use: Flowering shrub for indoors, a greenhouse, or a sunroom. Can be placed outdoors during summer if kept in a sunny, sheltered spot.

Origin: South America.

Plant description: Flowering shrub with oval, grass-green leaves, waxy in texture, and large, funnel-shaped, golden-yellow flowers. The plant has a milky sap.

Light and position: Prefers full sunlight; tolerates filtered sun.

Temperature range: Warm, cooler during winter. Tolerates temperatures down to 59°F (15°C).

Water: Water freely in the growing season, keeping the soil constantly moist. The plant tolerates a slight drying out, but this will result in smaller flowers.

Feeding: Feed with a low-nitrogen fertilizer every two weeks from spring to fall. Do not feed during the remainder of the year.

Special care: In fall, when flowering has stopped, the shrub can be cut back to promote a more bushy growth. Repot every year in early spring.

Pests and diseases: Aphids, mealy bugs, white fly, scale insects, and spider mites.

Other species/cultivars: The cultivar 'Hendersonii' has extra-large flowers. 'Silver Dwarf' is a compact cultivar with silver-green leaves. The species *A. neriifolia* has smaller flowers and oleander-like leaves. *A. blanchetii* has reddish-purple flowers.

Propagation: In spring, take softwood cuttings from new stem growth.

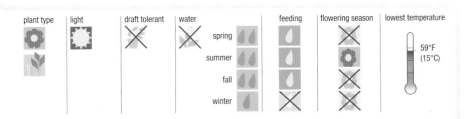

plant type	light	draft tolerant	water		feeding	flowering season	lowest temperature
			spring				
			summer				59°F (15°C)
			fall				
			winter				

Alocasia x *amazonica*
Alocasia/Elephant's Ear

Family: *Araceae*

Use: Sculptural foliage plant for indoors or outdoors in a shady spot in summer.

Plant description: Tuberous herb displaying very large, arrow-shaped, green leaves with veins and scalloped margins in contrasting white.

Light and position: Filtered sunlight to shade; avoid direct sunlight.

Temperature range: Warm, tolerating temperatures down to 59°F (15°C).

Water: Keep the soil constantly moist, as the plant does not tolerate drying out. It prefers high humidity, so mist frequently with a hand-spray.

Feeding: Feed with a low-nitrogen fertilizer once a month from spring to fall. Do not feed during the rest of the year.

Special care: Repot every year in spring.

Pests and diseases: Aphids, mealy bugs, scale insects, spider mites, and gray mold.

Other species/cultivars: Cultivars are 'Black Velvet,' with dark, velvety leaves; 'Calidora,' with very large, grass-green leaves; 'Polly,' with dark green leaves and contrasting white veins and margins.

Propagation: By rhizomes in spring.

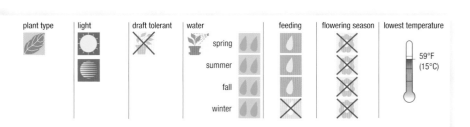

plant type	light	draft tolerant	water		feeding	flowering season	lowest temperature
			spring				
			summer				59°F (15°C)
			fall				
			winter				

plant type

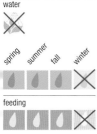

light

draft tolerant

water

spring summer fall winter

feeding

flowering season

lowest temperature

41°F
(5°C)

Aloe vera

Medicinal Aloe/

Bitter Aloe/Aloe Vera

Family: *Aloaceae*

Use: Sculptural succulent for indoors, or a greenhouse or sunroom in summer. Also a medicinal plant.

Origin: North Africa, East Africa, tropical Africa, South Africa, and Arabia.

Plant description: Succulent with a short stem and a rosette of fleshy leaves, edged with soft, pale spines. The leaves are spotted when young, and the flowers are yellow or orange.

Light and position: Full sunlight to filtered sun.

Temperature range: Warm, cooler during winter. Tolerates temperatures down to 41°F (5°C).

Water: Water regularly but sparingly from spring to fall. The soil should be kept almost dry in winter. Avoid letting water stand in the rosette.

Feeding: Feed with a low-nitrogen fertilizer once a month from spring to fall. Do not feed during the remainder of the year.

Special care: The plant needs a dormant period from October to April, when it should be kept in a light, cool position, at about 41°F (5°C). Repot every second or third year in early spring.

Pests and diseases: Aphids and spider mites.

Other species/cultivars: Many species are cultivated for indoor use. *A. mitriformis* has a compact rosette of broad, blue-green leaves with pale, horny teeth. *A. variegata* has an elongated rosette of dark green leaves with white spots arranged in bands.

Propagation: Separate the young plants during spring and summer. They can be planted in clumps or as single rosettes.

Anigozanthos

Kangaroo Paw/Cat's Paw/
Australian Sword Lily (hybrids)

Family: *Haemodoraceae*

Use: Flowering perennial for indoors, a greenhouse or sunroom, or outdoors from spring to fall. Rare.

Origin: Western Australia.

Plant description: Perennial herb with a thick rootstock and lance-shaped leaves. The erect inflorescence is dramatic, with woolly, tubular flowers. The flowers, red, orange, or yellow, are likened to kangaroo paws.

Light and position: Full sunlight to filtered sun.

Temperature range: Warm to cool, tolerating temperatures down to 41°F (5°C).

Water: Water regularly from spring to fall, more sparingly during the rest of the year.

Feeding: Feed with a low-nitrogen fertilizer once a month from spring to fall. Do not feed during the remainder of the year.

Special care: During winter the plant prefers to be kept dormant, in a light, cool position at about 41–50°F (5–10°C). Repot every second year in spring.

Pests and diseases: Leaf spot.

Other species/cultivars: A range of cultivars is available, varying in plant size and flower color.

Propagation: Plants can be divided in early spring.

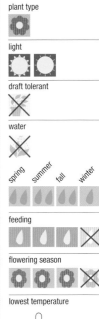

plant type

light

draft tolerant

water

spring summer fall winter

feeding

flowering season

lowest temperature

41°F
(5°C)

Anthurium andraeanum
Flamingo Flower/Tailflower

Family: *Araceae*

Use: Flowering plant for indoors.

Origin: Colombia.

Plant description: Erect herbaceous plant with long, stalked, shiny leaves shaped like hearts. The flowers are very showy, with a waxy spathe of brilliant red, pink, purple, yellow-green, or white surrounding a yellow or orange spadix.

Light and position: Tolerates a shady to filtered-sun position. Keep away from direct sunlight.

Temperature range: Warm. Tolerates temperatures down to 59°F (15°C), but prefers higher temperatures.

Water: Water regularly with soft water, and avoid letting the soil dry out. Mist frequently with a hand-spray to maintain high humidity.

Feeding: Feed with a low-nitrogen fertilizer once a month from spring to fall. Do not feed during the remainder of the year.

Special care: Repot every second year in spring.

Pests and diseases: Aphids, scale insects, spider mites, and gray mold.

Other species/cultivars: Many cultivars and species with varying shape, size, and color of spathe and spadix are sold as indoor plants. 'Champion' has a white spathe; 'Laura' has a shiny red spathe; 'Arinos' has a yellow-green and pink spathe. *A. clarinervium* has dark green leaves with prominent white veins and a small, light green spathe.

Propagation: Plants can be divided in early spring.

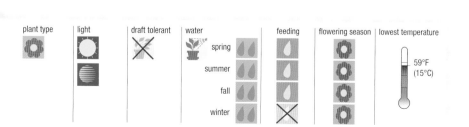

plant type	light	draft tolerant	water		feeding	flowering season	lowest temperature
			spring				59°F (15°C)
			summer				
			fall				
			winter				

Aphelandra squarrosa

Saffron Spike/Zebra Plant

Family: *Acanthaceae*

Use: Flowering plant for indoors, a greenhouse, or a sunroom.

Origin: Southeast Brazil.

Plant description: Compact plant with waxy, dark green leaves featuring prominent white veins. The colorful terminal spikes are composed of long-lasting, waxy, yellow bracts and yellow flowers.

Light and position: Filtered sunlight; keep away from full sun.

Temperature range: Warm to cool, tolerating temperatures down to 46°F (8°C).

Water: Water regularly, but more sparingly during winter when the plant is kept cool. Mist frequently with a hand-spray to maintain high humidity.

Feeding: Feed with a low-nitrogen fertilizer every two weeks from spring to fall. Do not feed during the remainder of the year.

Special care: After flowering, the plants can be cut back. Flower formation will be promoted if the plant is kept at 50°F (10°C) over eight weeks during winter. Repot every year in spring.

Pests and diseases: Aphids, scale insects, spider mites, and gray mold.

Other species/cultivars: The cultivar 'Dania' has a red-brown stem, very compact growth, and shiny dark green leaves with creamy veins.

Propagation: Take stem cuttings from greenwood in spring. The cuttings should be placed in a heated propagator or on a propagation blanket, with a bottom heat of 68–77°F (20–25°C).

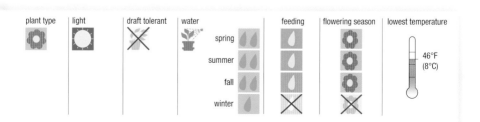

plant type	light	draft tolerant	water		feeding	flowering season	lowest temperature
				spring			
				summer			46°F (8°C)
				fall			
				winter			

Aporocactus (Disocactus) flagelliformis
Rat's Tail Cactus

Family: *Cactaceae*

Use: Flowering, sculptural cactus for indoors, a greenhouse, or a sunroom. Ideal for a hanging basket.

Origin: Mexico.

Plant description: Epiphytic cactus with slender stems that can reach a considerable height. The stems are studded with short tufts of bristly spines. The flowers are carmine-pink or cerise, and are followed by red berries.

Light and position: Prefers full sunlight; tolerates filtered sun.

Temperature range: Warm, cooler during winter. Tolerates temperatures down to 32°F (0°C).

Water: Water regularly during spring and summer, allowing the soil to dry out slightly before watering again. Water more sparingly from fall to spring.

Feeding: Feed with a low-nitrogen fertilizer once a month from spring to fall. Do not feed during the remainder of the year.

Special care: This plant is very easy to grow. It prefers a dormant period during winter, when it should be kept in a light, cool position at about 41–50°F (5–10°C). Repot every second or third year in early spring.

Pests and diseases: Mealy bugs, scale insects, and spider mites.

Other species/cultivars: None.

Propagation: Take stem cuttings from spring to summer.

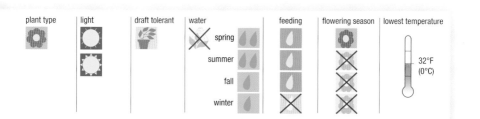

plant type	light	draft tolerant	water		feeding	flowering season	lowest temperature
			spring				
			summer				32°F (0°C)
			fall				
			winter				

Araucaria heterophylla
Norfolk Island Pine/House Pine
Family: *Araucariaceae*

Use: Sculptural foliage plant for indoors, a greenhouse, or a sunroom. Can be placed outside in a shady spot in summer.
Origin: Norfolk Island.
Plant description: Elegant evergreen tree with branches that grow parallel to the ground and soft, awl-shaped needles.
Light and position: Full sunlight to filtered sun.
Temperature range: Prefers a cool position, especially during winter. Tolerates temperatures down to 32°F (0°C).
Water: Water regularly with soft water, and avoid letting the soil dry out. Keep the soil drier during winter. The plant tolerates dry air.
Feeding: Feed with a low-nitrogen fertilizer once a month from spring to fall. Do not feed during the remainder of the year.
Special care: This plant prefers a dormant period during winter, when it should be kept in a light, cool position at about 41–50°F (5–10°C). Repot in a flat container every three or four years, in early spring.
Pests and diseases: Mealy bugs.
Other species/cultivars: None.
Propagation: Seeds can be sown in spring.

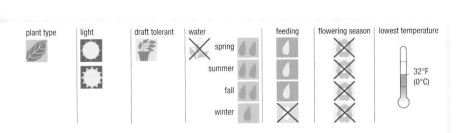

Ardisia crenata
Hen's Eye/Coralberry/
Spiceberry

Family: *Myrsinaceae*

Use: Ornamental plant for indoors, or a greenhouse or sunroom from spring to fall. Rare.

Origin: North India, China, Korea, Japan, and Taiwan.

Plant description: Small tree with thick, shiny, dark leaves, which are leathery in texture with crisped markings. The fragrant, white flowers are followed by waxy, red berries that will last nearly six months.

Light and position: Filtered sunlight. Avoid full sun as it may scorch the leaves.

Temperature range: Warm to cool, especially during winter. Tolerates temperatures down to 45°F (7°C).

Water: Water regularly, but more sparingly during winter. Avoid letting the soil dry out.

Feeding: Feed with a low-nitrogen fertilizer every two weeks from spring to fall. Do not feed during the remainder of the year.

Special care: This plant prefers a dormant period during winter, when it should be kept in a light, cool position at about 50–59°F (10–15°C). Repot and cut back every year in spring.

Pests and diseases: Mealy bugs, scale insects, and gray mold.

Other species/cultivars: None.

Propagation: Seeds are sown in spring; stem cuttings from semi-ripe shoots can be taken in fall.

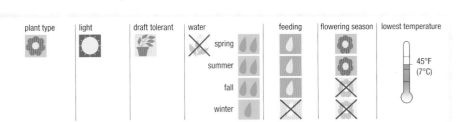

plant type	light	draft tolerant	water		feeding	flowering season	lowest temperature
			spring				
			summer				45°F (7°C)
			fall				
			winter				

Asparagus densiflorus

Asparagus Fern/
Foxtail Fern/
Emerald Fern

Family: *Asparagaceae*

Use: Tough ornamental foliage plant for indoors, a greenhouse, or a sunroom.

Origin: South Africa.

Plant description: Shrub with many branches and arching, pendulous stems covered with small grass-green "leaves" (not real leaves but cladophylls, leaves reduced to thorns). Red berries follow the small, fragrant, white flowers.

Light and position: Full to filtered sun.

Temperature range: Warm to cool (in winter). Tolerates temperatures down to 46°F (8°C).

Water: Water regularly from spring to fall, letting the soil dry out slightly before watering again. Keep the soil drier during the rest of the year. The tuberous roots of this plant enable it to tolerate drying out for a few weeks.

Feeding: Feed with a low-nitrogen fertilizer once a month from spring to fall. Do not feed during the remainder of the year.

Special care: The stems can be cut back to make the plant more compact. Sprinkle with water now and then to remove old "leaves." The plant prefers a dormant period during winter, when it should be kept in a light, cool position at about 50–59°F (10–15°C). Repot every third year in spring.

Pests and diseases: Aphids, spider mites, gray mold.

Other species/cultivars:
The stems of the cultivar 'Meyers' are more upright. 'Spregeri' has fluffier, arching stems. *A. falcatus* is an upright plant with narrow, sickle-shaped "leaves." *A. setaceus* has fern-like fronds of small, needle-shaped branches.

Propagation: Seeds or by plant division in early spring.

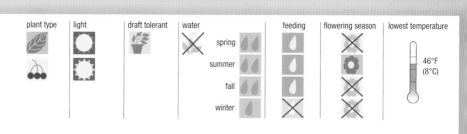

plant type	light	draft tolerant	water		feeding	flowering season	lowest temperature
			spring				46°F (8°C)
			summer				
			fall				
			winter				

Aspidistra elatior
Aspidistra/Cast-Iron Plant/
Bar-Room Plant
Family: *Convallariaceae*

Use: A sculptural foliage plant for indoors, a greenhouse, or a sunroom.
Origin: China.
Plant description: Tough plant with thick roots and large, shiny, dark green leaves, leathery in texture, with long stalks. Its rare, bell-shaped flowers, cream with a maroon interior, are found at ground level.
Light and position: Tolerates a shady position to filtered sun. Keep away from direct sunlight.
Temperature range: Cool, especially during winter. Tolerates temperatures down to 45°F (7°C).

Water: Water regularly, allowing the soil to dry out slightly before watering again. Water more sparingly during winter when the plant is kept cool. Tolerates dry air.
Feeding: Feed with a low-nitrogen fertilizer every two weeks from spring to fall. Do not feed during the remainder of the year.
Special care: Repot only when necessary, usually every three to four years, in early spring.
Pests and diseases: Mealy bugs, scale insects, and spider mites.
Other species/cultivars: The cultivar 'Variegata' has creamy white stripes running the length of its leaves.
Propagation: From plant division in spring.

plant type

light

draft tolerant

water

spring	summer	fall	winter

feeding

flowering season

lowest temperature

45°F (7°C)

light

draft tolerant

water

spring summer fall winter

feeding

flowering season

lowest temperature

50°F
(10°C)

Asplenium nidus
Bird's-Nest Fern

Family: *Aspleniaceae*

Use: A sculptural fern for indoors, or a greenhouse or sunroom in summer.
Origin: East Africa, tropical Asia, Australia, and Polynesia.
Plant description: Epiphytic fern with a very short rhizome bearing a simple rosette of lance-shaped, shiny leaves that form a "nest."
Light and position: Shade to filtered sunlight; keep away from full sun.
Temperature range: Warm to cool, tolerating temperatures down to 50°F (10°C).

Water: Water regularly, but more sparingly during winter. Tolerates a slight drying out.
Feeding: Feed with a low-nitrogen fertilizer once a month from spring to fall. Do not feed during the remainder of the year. Repot every second year in spring.
Special care: Prefers a humid, shady position. Mist frequently with a hand-spray.
Pests and diseases: Aphids, mealy bugs, scale insects, and gray mold.
Other species/cultivars: The species *A. antiquum* look similar, but the leaves have wavy margins.
Propagation: By spores.

Beaucarnea recurvata

Ponytail Palm/Elephant'sFoot/
Bottle Palm

Family: *Dracaenaceae*

Use: Tough, sculptural foliage plant for indoors, or a greenhouse or sunroom in summer.

Origin: Mexico.

Plant description: Tree-like plant with a circular or elongated woody trunk, swollen at the base. The pendulous, linear leaves are found in a rosette at the top of the stem.

Light and position: Full sunlight to filtered sun. Tolerates a shady position for a short period.

Temperature range: Warm, cooler during winter. Tolerates temperatures down to 41°F (5°C).

Water: Water regularly from spring to fall, letting the soil dry out before watering again. The plant can tolerate drying out for a month and should be watered more sparingly when it is kept cool. It also tolerates dry air.

Feeding: Feed with a low-nitrogen fertilizer once a month from spring to fall. Do not feed during the remainder of the year.

Special care: During winter, place in a light, cool position, at a temperature of about 50–59°F (10–15°C). Repot every three years in spring.

Pests and diseases: None.

Other species/cultivars: None.

Propagation: Seeds may be sown in spring.

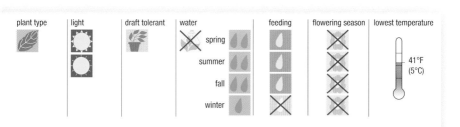

plant type	light	draft tolerant	water		feeding	flowering season	lowest temperature
				spring			
				summer			41°F (5°C)
				fall			
				winter			

Begonia elatior
Elatior Begonia/Winter-Flowering Begonia (hybrids)

Family: *Begoniaceae*

Use: Flowering ornamental for indoors, a greenhouse or sunroom, or outdoors during summer.

Plant description: Bushy herbaceous plant with large, dark green leaves. Flowers may be single or double and are found in a wide range of colors, including white, yellow, salmon, red, and purple.

Light and position: Filtered sun; keep away from full sunlight.

Temperature range: Warm to cool, tolerating temperatures down to 41°F (5°C).

Water: Water often from spring to summer, more sparingly during the rest of the year. The plant does not tolerate drying out.

Feeding: Feed with a low-nitrogen fertilizer once a month while in bud and flowering.

Special care: Keep the plant in a well-ventilated place to protect it from mildew. Discard after flowering.

Pests and diseases: Aphids, spider mites, gray mold, and mildew.

Other species/cultivars: Many cultivars, offering different flower colors, are available. Often sold at Christmas, cultivars of *B. lorraine* hybrids have clusters of smaller white, pink, or salmon flowers.

Propagation: From stem or tip cuttings taken in early spring.

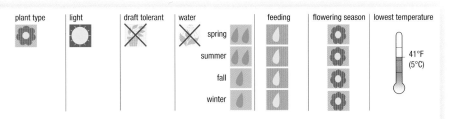

plant type	light	draft tolerant	water		feeding	flowering season	lowest temperature
			spring				
			summer				41°F (5°C)
			fall				
			winter				

Begonia rex
Rex Begonia/King Begonia/
Painted-Leaf Begonia

Family: *Begoniaceae*

Use: A foliage plant for indoors.

Origin: India.

Plant description: Bushy herbaceous plant with ornamental asymmetrical leaves, shaped like hearts and variegated in shades of pink, green, silver, red, purple, and brown.

Light and position: Filtered sunlight; keep away from full sun.

Temperature range: Warm to cool, tolerating temperatures down to 50°F (10°C).

Water: Water regularly from spring to fall, allowing the soil to dry out slightly before watering again. Water more sparingly during the rest of the year. Mist frequently with a hand-spray to maintain high humidity.

Feeding: Feed with a low-nitrogen fertilizer once a month from spring to fall. Do not feed during the remainder of the year.

Special care: Prefers high humidity, as mildew can be a problem in dry air. Repot every year in spring.

Pests and diseases: Aphids, spider mites, and gray mold.

Other species/cultivars: Many species and cultivars offering different leaf colors and sizes are available. *B. boweri* cultivars have smaller green and brown variegated leaves, with erect hairs along the margins and small white flowers.

Propagation: From leaf, stem, or tip cuttings taken in early spring.

plant type	light	draft tolerant	water		feeding	flowering season	lowest temperature
				spring			50°F (10°C)
				summer			
				fall			
				winter			

Bougainvillea glabra
Purple Bougainvillea/
Paper Flower

Family: *Nyctaginaceae*

Use: Flowering climber for indoors, a greenhouse or sunroom, or outdoors in summer. Ideal for a small trellis or training to a hoop.

Origin: Brazil.

Plant description: Strong, flowering climber that scrambles by means of curved thorns found in the leaf axils of its bright green leaves. Vivid bracts in shades of purple, pink, yellow, or white surround insignificant white flowers.

Light and position: Prefers full sunlight; tolerates filtered sun.

Temperature range: Warm to cool, preferring a cool position in winter. Tolerates temperatures down to 41°F (5°C).

Water: This plant will rot and die if overwatered. Water regularly in growing season, allowing the soil to dry out before watering again, but very sparingly during winter if the plant is kept cool.

Feeding: Feed with a low-nitrogen fertilizer every two weeks from spring to fall. Do not feed during the remainder of the year.

Special care: The plant needs support, such as a trellis or hoop. Cut back long shoots in fall, and allow the plant a dormant period during winter, keeping it in a light, cool position, at about 41–54°F (5–12°C). Repot every year in spring.

Pests and diseases: Aphids, mealy bugs, scale insects, spider mites, white fly, and gray mold.

Other species/cultivars: There are many cultivars, varying in size and color of leaf and bract. 'Alexandra' has small, shiny leaves and dark purple bracts. 'Dania' has larger leaves and clusters of smaller, purplish-red bracts. 'Vera Deep Purple' has larger leaves and light purple bracts.

Propagation: In summer, take stem cuttings from softwood or from semi-ripe shoots with a section of last year's growth.

plant type	light	draft tolerant	water		feeding	flowering season	lowest temperature
				spring			
				summer			41°F (5°C)
				fall			
				winter			

plant type

light

draft tolerant

✕

water

✕

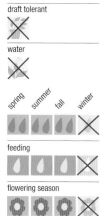

spring summer fall winter

feeding

flowering season

lowest temperature

59°F
(15°C)

Bouvardia
Bouvardia (hybrids)

Family: *Rubiaceae*

Use: Flowering ornamental for indoors, or a greenhouse or sunroom in summer.

Plant description: Bushy flowering shrub with waxy leaves growing in opposite pairs on the stem and clusters of tubular flowers, which may be pink *(below left)*, red *(below right)*, lilac, or white *(left)*. The flower buds resemble small balloons.

Light and position: Prefers full sunlight; tolerates filtered sun.

Temperature range: Warm to cool, tolerating temperatures down to 59°F (15°C).

Water: Keep the soil constantly moist when the plant is flowering. It does not tolerate drying out.

Feeding: Feed with a low-nitrogen fertilizer every two weeks when flowering. Do not feed during the remainder of the year.

Special care: Cut off old flower clusters to promote the formation of new flowers. Discard the plant when flowering has finished.

Pests and diseases: Aphids, spider mites, white fly, gray mold, and mildew.

Other species/cultivars: There is a range of cultivars, offering different flower colors.

Propagation: Take cuttings from the top of the stem in spring. The cuttings should be placed in a heated propagator or on a propagation blanket, with a bottom heat of 68–72°F (20–22°C).

Brugmansia sanguinea
Red Angel's Trumpet

Family: *Solanaceae*

Use: Flowering shrub for indoors, a greenhouse or sunroom, or outdoors in summer.

Origin: Colombia, Ecuador, Peru, and northern Chile.

Plant description: Tree-like shrub with large oval leaves, which have a velvety, hairy texture. The nodding tubular flowers have a green calyx and a yellow, red, or orange corolla.

Light and position: Enjoys filtered sunlight; keep away from full sun.

Temperature range: Warm to cool, preferring a cool position in winter. Tolerates temperatures down to 41°F (5°C).

Water: Water regularly in growing season, allowing the soil to dry out slightly before watering again, but very sparingly during winter if the plant is kept cool. This plant will not flower if it is watered too much, but it does not tolerate drying out when flowering.

Feeding: Feed with a low-nitrogen fertilizer every two weeks from spring to fall. Do not feed during the remainder of the year.

Special care: Cut back long shoots in fall. The plant needs a dormant period during winter, when it should be kept dry and cool, at 41°F–50°F (5°C–10°C). Repot in spring, cut back long shoots, and start watering again.

Pests and diseases: Mealy bugs, scale insects, and spider mites.

Other species/cultivars: Many cultivars, hybrids, and species are cultivated. The most common are *B.* x *candida*, which has pendulous, fragrant, white flowers; the smaller shrub *B. arborea*, with fragrant white flowers; *B. aurea*, with night-scented white or golden-yellow flowers; and *B. suaveolens*, which is a large shrub with night-scented white flowers.

Propagation: Stem cuttings from softwood and greenwood are taken in spring and summer.

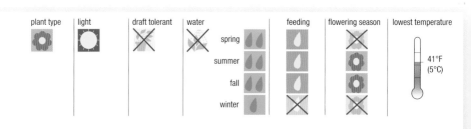

plant type	light	draft tolerant	water		feeding	flowering season	lowest temperature
				spring			
				summer			41°F (5°C)
				fall			
				winter			

Caladium bicolor
Elephant's Ear/
Heart of Jesus/Angel Wings

Family: *Araceae*

Use: Foliage plant for indoors, or outdoors in a shady spot in summer.

Origin: Ecuador.

Plant description: Tuberous, herbaceous perennial featuring heart-shaped leaves, brightly blotched with pink, white, purple, cream, or yellow-green.

Light and position: Filtered sunlight. The plant should be kept away from full sun, but a shady position will result in a paler leaf color.

Temperature range: Warm, tolerating temperatures down to 64°F (18°C).

Water: Water regularly in growing season, allowing the soil to dry out before watering again. Do not water during the dormant period. The plant will die if overwatered, but should be misted frequently with a hand-spray to maintain high humidity.

Feeding: Feed with a low-nitrogen fertilizer every two weeks from spring to fall. Do not feed during the remainder of the year.

Special care: The plant needs a rest period during winter. Stop watering in fall, when the plant starts to die down. Keep the tubers dry and at a temperature of about 64°F (18°C) throughout the winter. Repot the tubers in early spring and start watering again.

Pests and diseases: Aphids and spider mites.

Other species/cultivars: Many different hybrids and cultivars offer a wide range of leaf colors.

Propagation: By plant division in spring.

plant type	light	draft tolerant	water		feeding	flowering season	lowest temperature
				spring			
				summer			64°F (18°C)
				fall			
				winter			

plant type

light

draft tolerant

water

spring   summer   fall   winter

feeding

flowering season

lowest temperature

64°F
(18°C)

Calathea roseopicta
Calathea

Family: *Marantaceae*

Use: A foliage plant for indoors.
Origin: Brazil.
Plant description: Compact herb with rounded, short-stalked leaves. The leaves are colored dark olive-green, with a red midrib, areas of bright red near the margins, and a purple underside.
Light and position: Filtered sunlight; keep away from full sun.
Temperature range: Warm, tolerating temperatures down to 64°F (18°C).
Water: Keep the soil constantly moist, as the plant does not tolerate drying out. It prefers high humidity, so mist frequently with a hand-spray.

Feeding: Feed with a low-nitrogen fertilizer once a month from spring to fall. Do not feed during the remainder of the year.
Special care: Repot every second or third year in spring.
Pests and diseases: Spider mites.
Other species/cultivars: Many species and cultivars are bred for indoor use. *C. makoyana* have long-stalked leaves with feathery patterns of olive- and yellow-green. *C. rufibarba* has long, oval leaves with wavy margins and dark purple stalks. *C. zebrina* is a taller plant with dark green patches on either side of the midrib.
Propagation: Divide the plant in late spring.

Callistemon citrinus
Crimson Bottlebrush

75

Family: *Myrtaceae*

Use: Tough flowering shrub for indoors, a greenhouse, or a sunroom. Can be placed outdoors in summer.

Origin: Australia.

Plant description: Small tree or weeping shrub with stiff, linear leaves and "bottle-brush" flowers, which have a mass of crimson brush-like stamens and yellow anthers. The leaves have a lemon scent when crushed.

Light and position: Prefers full sunlight; tolerates filtered sun.

Temperature range: Warm, cooler during winter. Tolerates temperatures down to 32°F (0°C) and dry air.

Water: This plant will rot and die if overwatered. Water regularly with soft water from spring to fall, allowing the soil to dry out slightly before watering again. Water more sparingly during the rest of the year.

Feeding: Feed with a low-nitrogen fertilizer once a month from spring to fall. Do not feed during the remainder of the year.

Special care: The plant needs a dormant period during winter, when it should be kept in a light, cool position, at about 41°F (5°C). Repot every year in early spring, and cut back after flowering.

Pests and diseases: Fungus disease.

Other species/cultivars: 'Splendens' has large, broad leaves and deep-red flower spikes. 'Jeffersi' is a Californian variety with broad, short leaves and purplish flowers.

Propagation: Stem cuttings from greenwood to semi-ripe shoots can be taken in summer and fall.

plant type

light

draft tolerant

water

spring summer fall winter

feeding

flowering season

lowest temperature

32°F
(0°C)

Campanula/Carpathian Harebell/
Tussock Bellflower

Family: *Campanulaceae*

Use: Flowering herbaceous plant for indoors, a greenhouse or sunroom, or outdoors from spring to fall. A tough perennial in the garden.

Origin: Europe.

Plant description: Compact perennial herb with heart-shaped leaves and attractively bell-shaped single or double flowers, which may be white or blue.

Light and position: Full sunlight to filtered sun.

Temperature range: Prefers a cool position, tolerating temperatures down to 32°F (0°C).

Water: Keep the soil moist, especially during summer. This plant does not tolerate drying out.

Feeding: Feed with a low-nitrogen fertilizer once a month from spring to fall. Do not feed during the remainder of the year.

Special care: Remove old flowers to allow space for new buds. Discard after flowering or plant out in the garden.

Pests and diseases: Aphids, spider mites, white fly, mildew, and gray mold.

Other species/cultivars: 'Thorpedo Blue Ball' has double flowers. *C. isophylla* has single, star-like flowers, in white or blue. *C. portenschlagiana* 'Get Me' has pendant shoots with heart-shaped leaves and a mass of bell-shaped flowers in purplish blue. *C. poscharskyana* has pendant shoots and star-like, bluish flowers with a white center.

Propagation: Take stem-tip cuttings from new growth after flowering.

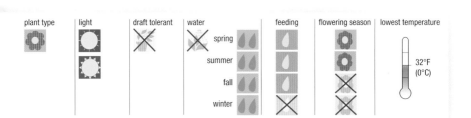

Capsicum annuum

Ornamental Pepper/
Paprika/Green Pepper/Red Pepper/Sweet Pepper

Family: *Solanaceae*

Use: Ornamental pepper for indoors, a greenhouse or sunroom, or outdoors in summer. The fruit may be grown for culinary use.

Origin: Mexico.

Plant description: Compact, herbaceous annual with lance-shaped, dark green leaves. Small, white flowers are followed by ornamental peppers in strong colors. The peppers change color as they mature.

Light and position: Prefers full sunlight; tolerates filtered sun.

Temperature range: Warm to cool, tolerating temperatures down to 41°F (5°C).

Water: This plant will rot and die if overwatered. Water regularly, allowing the soil to dry out slightly before watering again.

Feeding: Feed with a low-nitrogen fertilizer once a month from spring to fall. Do not feed during the remainder of the year.

Special care: Discard after fruiting.

Pests and diseases: Aphids and gray mold.

Other species/cultivars: Different cultivars offering a range of sizes and colors of pepper are available.

Propagation: Dry the peppers and sow the seeds in spring.

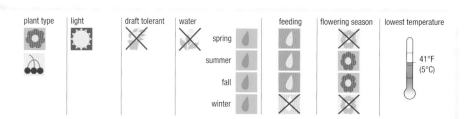

plant type	light	draft tolerant	water		feeding	flowering season	lowest temperature
			spring				
			summer				41°F (5°C)
			fall				
			winter				

Cereus peruvianus

Peruvian Cactus/Peruvian Apple Cactus

Family: *Cactaceae*

Use: Sculptural cactus for indoors, a greenhouse, or sunroom. If placed nearby, this plant is said to neutralize harmful radiation from computers, televisions, and mobile phones.

Origin: South America, naturalized in southeast Florida.

Plant description: Fleshy, columnar, ribbed cactus growing shiny, dark green branches with a few brown spines.

Light and position: Prefers full sunlight; tolerates filtered sun.

Temperature range: Warm, but cooler during winter when the plant tolerates temperatures down to 41°F (5°C).

Water: Water regularly, allowing the soil to dry out slightly before watering again. Water more sparingly from fall to spring, and keep the soil dry during winter if the plant is kept cool.

Feeding: Feed with a low-nitrogen fertilizer once a month from spring to fall. Do not feed during the remainder of the year.

Special care: This plant is very easy to grow. It enjoys cooler temperatures during winter, when it should be kept at 50–59°F (10–15°C). Repot every second or third year in early spring.

Pests and diseases: Mealy bugs, scale insects, and spider mites.

Other species/cultivars: The cultivar 'Monstrosus' forms flat, irregular heads.

Propagation: Stem cuttings can be taken from spring through summer. Let them dry out for a few days before potting.

plant type

light

draft tolerant

water

spring summer fall winter

feeding

flowering season

lowest temperature

41°F
(5°C)

Rosary Vine/Hearts on a String/
Hearts Entangled/Sweetheart Vine

Family: *Asclepiadaceae*

Use: Trailing succulent for indoors, a greenhouse, or a sunroom.

Origin: South Africa and Zimbabwe.

Plant description: Succulent with trailing, filamentous branches bearing tubes at the nodes. The heart-shaped, dark green leaves are marbled, with a silver and purple underside, and the flowers are purplish.

Light and position: Prefers full sunlight; tolerates filtered sun.

Temperature range: Warm, cooler during winter. Tolerates temperatures down to 32°F (0°C).

Water: This plant will rot and die if overwatered. Water regularly but sparingly from spring to fall, and keep the soil almost dry in winter.

Feeding: Feed with a low-nitrogen fertilizer once a month from spring to fall. Do not feed during the remainder of the year.

Special care: Avoid standing the plant in water. It prefers a dormant period during winter, when it should be kept in a light, cool position at about 41–50°F (5–10°C). Repot every third year in spring.

Pests and diseases: Aphids and spider mites.

Other species/cultivars: *C. sandersonii* has small, oval leaves and upright, green flowers that resemble parachutes.

Propagation: From stem-tubers or cuttings taken from spring to fall.

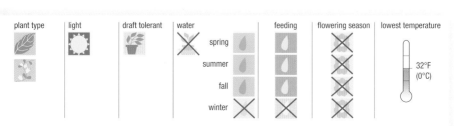

plant type	light	draft tolerant	water		feeding	flowering season	lowest temperature
			spring				
			summer				32°F (0°C)
			fall				
			winter				

Chamaedorea elegans
Parlor Palm

Family: *Arecaceae*

Use: A sculptural palm for indoors, or a greenhouse or sunroom in summer.
Origin: Mexico and Guatemala.
Plant description: Small, elegant palm with clusters of thin stems and spirally arranged, dark green, pinnate leaves. It produces yellow to black fruit.
Light and position: Tolerates a shady position to filtered sun. Keep the plant away from direct sunlight.
Temperature range: Warm to cool, tolerating temperatures down to 50°F (10°C).
Water: Keep the soil constantly moist, especially during summer. The plant does not tolerate drying out.
Feeding: Feed with a low-nitrogen fertilizer once a month from spring to fall. Do not feed during the remainder of the year.
Special care: Too much light may result in yellow leaves. Repot every year in spring.
Pests and diseases: Mealy bugs, scale insects, and spider mites.
Other species/cultivars: *C. costaricana* has dark green canes, resembling bamboo, and larger pinnate leaves.
Propagation: Seeds are sown in spring.

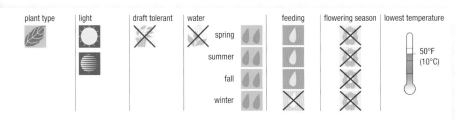

plant type	light	draft tolerant	water		feeding	flowering season	lowest temperature
				spring			
				summer			50°F (10°C)
				fall			
				winter			

Chlorophytum comosum
Spider Plant

Family: *Anthericaceae*

Use: Tough foliage plant for indoors, a greenhouse, or a sunroom. Ideal as groundcover or in a hanging basket.

Origin: South Africa.

Plant description: Perennial rosette plant growing long, narrow, grass-like leaves with white-banded centers. Pendant plantlets develop from long racemes of white flowers.

Light and position: Prefers filtered sunlight. Keep this plant away from full sun.

Temperature range: Warm, but cooler during winter when the plant tolerates temperatures down to 41°F (5°C).

Water: Water well from spring to fall, although the plant will tolerate drying out. Keep the soil drier if the plant is kept cool during winter. Mist frequently with a hand-spray to maintain high humidity.

Feeding: Feed with a low-nitrogen fertilizer once a month from spring to fall. Do not feed during the remainder of the year.

Special care: This plant prefers high humidity. It enjoys cooler temperatures during winter, when it should be kept at 50–59°F (10–15°C). Repot every second year in early spring.

Pests and diseases: Spider mites.

Other species/cultivars: A few cultivars are available, varying mainly in leaf shape and in the color of the banded center.

Propagation: Repot rooting plantlets at any time of year.

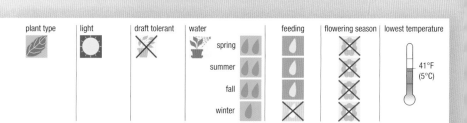

plant type	light	draft tolerant	water		feeding	flowering season	lowest temperature
				spring			41°F (5°C)
				summer			
				fall			
				winter			

plant type

light

draft tolerant

water

spring   summer   fall   winter

feeding

flowering season

lowest temperature

41°F
(5°C)

Chrysalidocarpus lutescens

Butterfly Palm/Madagascar Palm/
Yellow Palm/Areca Palm/Cane Palm/
Golden Yellow Palm

Family: *Arecaceae*

Use: A sculptural palm for indoors, or a greenhouse or sunroom in summer.

Origin: Madagascar.

Plant description: Tall, bushy palm displaying yellowish stems and yellow-green pinnate leaves with furrowed stalks dotted with black.

Light and position: Tolerates a shady to filtered-sun position. Keep away from direct sunlight.

Temperature range: Warm to cool, tolerating temperatures down to 41°F (5°C).

Water: Keep the soil constantly moist, especially during summer. This plant does not tolerate drying out.

Feeding: Feed with a low-nitrogen fertilizer once a month from spring to fall. Do not feed during the remainder of the year.

Special care: Repot every year in spring.

Pests and diseases: Mealy bugs, scale insects, and spider mites.

Other species/cultivars: None.

Propagation: Seeds are sown in spring.

Cissus striata
Miniature Grape Ivy/
Ivy of Paraguay

Family: *Vitaceae*

Use: Foliage climber for indoors, a greenhouse or sunroom, or outdoors in summer. Ideal for a small trellis.

Origin: Chile and South Brazil.

Plant description: Small climber with thin, reddish shoots that scramble up using tiny tendrils. The small, palmate leaves comprise five oval leaflets, toothed toward the apex.

Light and position: Full sunlight to filtered sun.

Temperature range: Warm to cool, tolerating temperatures down to 32°F (0°C).

Water: Water regularly from spring to fall, more sparingly during winter. Avoid letting the soil dry out.

Feeding: Feed with a low-nitrogen fertilizer every two weeks from spring to fall. Do not feed during the remainder of the year.

Special care: Repot every second year in spring. Avoid sudden large changes in temperature.

Pests and diseases: Aphids, spider mites, and white fly.

Other species/cultivars: *C. antarctica* has oval leaves, irregularly toothed; *C. discolor* has beautiful reddish-blotched leaves; and *C. rhombifolia* has compound leaves with three leaflets.

Propagation: Stem cuttings from softwood or semi-ripe shoots can be taken at any time of year.

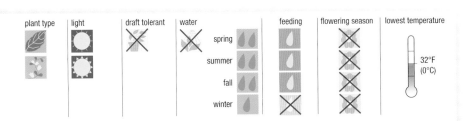

plant type	light	draft tolerant	water		feeding	flowering season	lowest temperature
				spring			
				summer			32°F (0°C)
				fall			
				winter			

Citrus limon
Common lemon

Family: *Rutaceae*

Use: Small fruit tree for indoors, a greenhouse or sunroom, or outdoors in summer. The fruit may be grown for culinary use.

Origin: North Myanmar and South China.

Plant description: Small, spiny tree with long, oval leaves. The white flowers have a beautiful scent and are followed by green lemons that turn yellow when ripe.

Light and position: Prefers full sunlight; tolerates filtered sun.

Temperature range: Warm to cool, tolerating temperatures down to 32°F (0°C).

Water: Water regularly from spring to fall, allowing the soil to dry out slightly before watering again. Keep the soil almost dry in winter.

Feeding: Feed with a low-nitrogen fertilizer once a month from spring to fall. Do not feed during the remainder of the year.

Special care: The plant needs a dormant period from October to April, when it should be kept in a light, cool position, at about 41°F (5°C). It also requires good drainage. Repot every year in spring.

Pests and diseases: Spider mites.

Other species/cultivars: A variety of cultivars can be found. 'Villa Franca' is an almost thornless tree, with medium to large fruit. 'Imperial' has very large fruit. 'Ponderosa' is a dwarf tree, with large flowers and fruit.

Propagation: From seeds in spring, or from stem cuttings taken from semi-ripe shoots in summer.

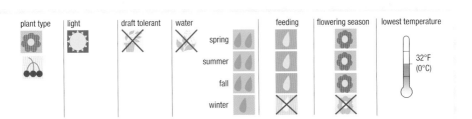

plant type	light	draft tolerant	water		feeding	flowering season	lowest temperature
			spring				
			summer				32°F (0°C)
			fall				
			winter				

plant type

light

draft tolerant

water

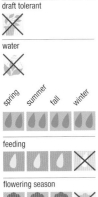

spring summer fall winter

feeding

flowering season

lowest temperature

14°F
(-10°C)

Clematis florida
Florida Clematis (hybrids)

Family: *Ranunculaceae*

Use: Flowering climber for indoors, a greenhouse, a sunroom, or outdoors. Ideal for a small trellis.

Origin: China.

Plant description: Climbing plant with double, pinnate, evergreen leaves. The flowers can be white *(left)*, bluish violet, purple *(below left)*, or bicolored white with violet or lilac anthers *(below right)*.

Light and position: Full to filtered sun.

Temperature range: Warm to cool, tolerating temperatures down to 14°F (minus 10°C). Frost-hardy in the garden.

Water: Keep the soil constantly moist, especially in a sunny position. When flowering, the plant should not dry out, but water more moderately during the rest of the year.

Feeding: Feed with a low-nitrogen fertilizer every two weeks from spring to fall. Do not feed during the remainder of the year.

Special care: Needs support, such as a small trellis. In fall, after flowering, the plant can be pruned to promote the formation of new growth. During the winter resting period, place it in a light, cool position, at about 41–50°F (5–10°C). Repot every year in spring.

Pests and diseases: Aphids and mildew.

Other species/cultivars: Different cultivars display various flower colors, ranging from white to lilac, bluish violet, and purple. Some have bicolored flowers with white or lilac anthers.

Propagation: Stem cuttings from softwood can be taken from spring to midsummer, and from semi-ripe shoots from mid to late summer.

Clerodendrum thomsoniae
Bleeding-Heart Vine/Bag Flower

Family: *Verbenaceae*

Use: Flowering climber for indoors, a greenhouse, or a sunroom. Ideal for a trellis.

Origin: West Africa and Cameroon.

Plant description: Climbing shrub with oval, dark green leaves and clusters of flowers. The flowers display an inflated calyx, colored pure white to pink, and a deep crimson corolla.

Light and position: Filtered sunlight; keep away from full sun.

Temperature range: Prefers a warm position, tolerating temperatures down to 50°F (10°C).

Water: Keep the soil constantly moist. Drying out should be avoided.

Feeding: Feed with a low-nitrogen fertilizer every two weeks from spring to fall. Do not feed during the remainder of the year.

Special care: Clerodendrum require good drainage, and the larger plants will need support, such as a trellis. Avoid large changes in temperature, which will make the flower buds drop. Repot every year in spring.

Pests and diseases: Aphids, spider mites, and white fly.

Other species/cultivars: Other cultivated hybrids and species are *C. x speciosum*, which has red flowers; *C. ugandense*, with blue flowers that resemble small butterflies; and *C. wallichii*, with pendent spikes of white flowers.

Propagation: Tip or stem cuttings can be taken in spring. The cuttings should be placed in a heated propagator or on a propagation blanket, with a bottom heat of 68–77°F (20–25°C).

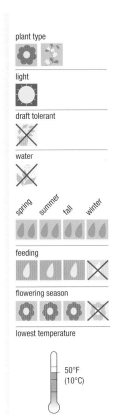

plant type

light

draft tolerant

water

spring · summer · fall · winter

feeding

flowering season

lowest temperature

50°F (10°C)

Clivia/Kaffir Lily

Family: *Amaryllidaceae*

Use: Flowering perennial for indoors, a greenhouse, or a sunroom.

Origin: South Africa.

Plant description: Herbaceous plant with fleshy roots and long, shiny, strap-like leaves. The bell-shaped flowers, colored orange and red, are clustered in a large umbel and are followed by red berries.

Light and position: Filtered sun. Keep the plant away from full sunlight.

Temperature range: Warm to cool, tolerating temperatures down to 32°F (0°C).

Water: Water regularly after flowering, allowing the soil to dry out slightly before watering again. From October, water more sparingly, keeping the soil almost dry. Start watering regularly again in early spring, when the flower buds become visible.

Feeding: Feed with a low-nitrogen fertilizer once a month from after flowering to fall. Do not feed during the remainder of the year.

Special care: Flower formation is induced by a rest period during winter, when the plant should be kept in a light, cool position, at about 50–59°F (10–15°C). Avoid direct sun, which may scorch the leaves. The plant needs good drainage and should be repotted every year in spring.

Pests and diseases: Spider mites.

Other species/cultivars: None.

Propagation: Seeds may be sown in spring, or the plant may be divided when not in flower.

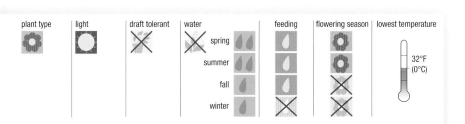

plant type	light	draft tolerant	water		feeding	flowering season	lowest temperature
			spring				32°F (0°C)
			summer				
			fall				
			winter				

Codiaeum variegatum
Codiaeum/Croton

Family: *Euphorbiaceae*

Use: Ornamental foliage plant for indoors, or a greenhouse or sunroom in summer.

Origin: Moluccas Islands.

Plant description: Compact shrub with highly ornamental leaves of varying shape. The leaves often feature vivid yellow or orange blotches.

Light and position:
Prefers full sunlight; tolerates filtered sun. A shady position will result in paler leaf color.

Temperature range: Prefers a warm position, tolerating temperatures down to 59°F (15°C).

Water: Water regularly all year. Avoid letting the soil dry out, especially if the plant is placed in full sun.

Feeding: Feed with a low-nitrogen fertilizer every two weeks from spring to fall. Do not feed during the remainder of the year.

Special care: Avoid low light, which may result in leaf drop. Repot every year in spring.

Pests and diseases: Aphids, mealy bugs, scale insects, and spider mites.

Other species/cultivars: There are many cultivars available, offering different shapes and colors of leaf.

The cultivar 'Aucubaefolia' has glossy, elliptic leaves with green-yellow blotches. 'Gold Star' has narrow, elongated leaves with yellow-green blotches. 'Petra' has larger, broader leaves with veins in yellow and orange.

Propagation: Take tip or stem cuttings from softwood or greenwood at any time of year. The cuttings should be placed in a heated propagator or on a propagation blanket, with a bottom heat of 68–77°F (20–25°C).

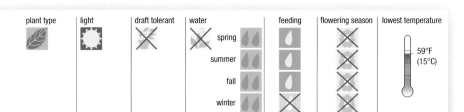

plant type	light	draft tolerant	water		feeding	flowering season	lowest temperature
			spring				
			summer				59°F (15°C)
			fall				
			winter				

plant type

light

draft tolerant

water

feeding

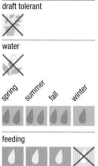

flowering season

lowest temperature

59°F
(15°C)

Coffea arabica
Arabian Coffee

Family: *Rubiaceae*

Use: Coffee tree for indoors, or a greenhouse or sunroom in summer.

Origin: Ethiopia and Sudan.

Plant description: Small tree with shiny, dark green leaves, elliptic in shape and featuring wavy margins. The fragrant, white flowers are gathered in terminal clusters and are followed by green berries, which later turn crimson.

Light and position: Filtered sunlight to shade; avoid direct sunlight.

Temperature range: Prefers a warm position, tolerating temperatures down to 59°F (15°C).

Water: Water frequently from spring to fall, more sparingly during the rest of the year. Avoid letting the soil dry out.

Feeding: Feed with a low-nitrogen fertilizer once a month from spring to fall. Do not feed during the remainder of the year.

Special care: Flower formation is induced by a rest period during winter, when the plant should be kept in a light, cool position, at about 59–64°F (15–18°C). Older plants (more than two or three years old) can be cut back and should also be repotted every year in spring.

Pests and diseases: Mealy bugs, scale insects, and spider mites.

Other species/cultivars: None.

Propagation: Seeds may be sown in spring.

Columnea
Columnea/Goldfish Plant (hybrids)

Family: *Gesneriaceae*

Use: Flowering trailer for indoors, or a greenhouse or sunroom in summer; ideal for hanging baskets.

Plant description: Epiphytic trailer with small, oval leaves and tubular flowers that may be yellow, orange, or red.

Light and position: Filtered sunlight. Keep the plant away from full sun.

Temperature range: Warm to cool, tolerating temperatures down to 54°F (12°C).

Water: Keep the soil constantly moist when the plant is flowering. Water regularly when it is not flowering, allowing the soil to dry out slightly before watering again.

Feeding: Feed with a low-nitrogen fertilizer once a month in the warmer months. Do not feed during the remainder of the year.

Special care: This is a good plant for a hanging basket. Repot every year in spring.

Pests and diseases: Spider mites.

Other species/cultivars: The cultivar 'Hostag' has orange flowers and small yellow-green leaves. 'Krakatau' and 'Sanne' have a more erect growth and orange flowers.

Propagation: Take tip cuttings or stem cuttings with two pairs of leaves at any time. The cuttings should be placed in a heated propagator or on a propagation blanket, with a bottom heat of 68–77°F (20–25°C).

plant type

light

draft tolerant

water

spring   summer   fall   winter

feeding

flowering season

lowest temperature

54°F (12°C)

Jade Plant/
Dollar Plant/Jade Tree

Family: *Crassulaceae*

Use: Tough, sculptural succulent for indoors, or a greenhouse or sunroom in summer.

Origin: South Africa.

Plant description: Succulent, branching shrub with glossy, fleshy leaves, spatulate in shape, which turn red in sun. Older plants produce pinkish-white flowers.

Light and position: Prefers full sunlight; tolerates filtered sun.

Temperature range: Warm, cooler during winter. Tolerates temperatures down to 32°F (0°C).

Water: This plant will rot and die if overwatered. Water regularly from spring to fall, allowing the soil to dry out before watering again. Keep the soil almost dry in winter.

Feeding: Feed with a low-nitrogen fertilizer once a month from spring to fall. Do not feed during the remainder of the year.

Special care: The plant needs a dormant period during winter, when it should be kept in a light, cool position, at about 41°F (5°C). Repot every third year in spring.

Pests and diseases: Aphids and spider mites.

Other species/cultivars: Many others species and cultivars of *Crassula* are cultivated. The cultivar 'Horn Tree' has erect, elongated, fleshy leaves. *C. coccinea* has upright branches tipped with dark red flowers.

Propagation: Take tip cuttings at any time of year.

plant type	light	draft tolerant	water		feeding	flowering season	lowest temperature
			spring				
			summer				32°F (0°C)
			fall				
			winter				

Cycas revoluta
Sago Palm/Cycad
Family: *Cycadaceae*

Use: A sculptural foliage plant for indoors, a greenhouse or sunroom, or outdoors in summer.

Origin: South Japan and Ryukyu Islands.

Plant description: Tough, tree-like plant with a stout, cylindrical trunk and dark green, pinnate leaves with a leathery texture. This plant is extremely slow-growing.

Light and position: Full sunlight to filtered sun.

Temperature range: Warm, cooler during winter. Tolerates temperatures down to 32°F (0°C).

Water: Water regularly from spring to fall, allowing the soil to dry out before watering again. The soil should be almost dry in winter if the plant is kept cool.

Feeding: Feed with a low-nitrogen fertilizer once a month from spring to fall. Do not feed during the remainder of the year.

Special care: Keep in a sheltered spot if placed outdoors. If the plant is kept in a sunny position, the leaves will grow larger. During winter it prefers a dormant period, in a light, cool position at about 41–50°F (5–10°C). Repot every third year in early spring.

Pests and diseases: Scale insects.

Other species/cultivars: None.

Propagation: Seeds may be sown in spring.

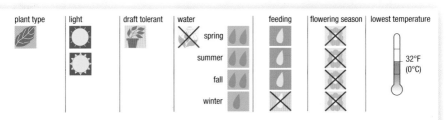

plant type	light	draft tolerant	water		feeding	flowering season	lowest temperature
			spring				
			summer				32°F (0°C)
			fall				
			winter				

Cyclamen persicum
Florist's Cyclamen
Family: *Primulaceae*

Use: Flowering perennial for indoors, a greenhouse or sunroom, or outdoors in summer.

Origin: Europe.

Plant description: Tuberous, herbaceous plant with heart-shaped leaves, colored blue-green with silver variegation. The nodding flowers can be different shades of white, salmon pink, red, or purple, and sometimes show a darker eye. The petals may be simple or feature frills and ruffles.

Light and position: Filtered sunlight. Keep the plant away from full sun.

Temperature range: Prefers a cool position, tolerating temperatures down to 46°F (8°C).

Water: Do not water the soil directly, but stand the pot in water for ten minutes. Water regularly, allowing the soil to dry out slightly before watering again. Water more sparingly if the plant is kept cool.

Feeding: None.

Special care: Deadhead regularly, removing any stalk stumps as these are prone to rotting. After flowering, the plant needs a dormant period, preferably in a sheltered spot in the garden, or in a cool position indoors, at a temperature of about 59°F (15°C). If the plant is kept in the garden, take it indoors before the temperature drops below about 46°F (8°C). Keep the soil drier during this period. Repot every year in fall.

Pests and diseases: Aphids and mildew.

Other species/cultivars: There are many cultivars, with a variety of flower shapes, colors, and sizes. Some cultivars have fragrant flowers.

Propagation: Seeds can be sown from midsummer to late winter.

plant type

light

draft tolerant

water

spring summer fall winter

feeding

flowering season

lowest temperature

46°F (8°C)

Cymbidium
Cymbidium Orchid (hybrids)

Family: *Orchidaceae*

Use: Flowering orchid for indoors, a greenhouse, or a sunroom.

Plant description: Tall orchid with elongated, grassy leaves and long-lasting waxy flowers clustered in arching racemes. Flowers may be colored green, yellow, pink, or white, usually with beautiful speckles or other markings.

Light and position: Filtered sunlight. Keep the plant away from full sun.

Temperature range: Warm to cool, tolerating temperatures down to 50°F (10°C).

Water: Water regularly with soft water and allow the soil to dry out slightly before watering again. Avoid standing water around bulbs and roots, which may result in fungus disease.

Feeding: Feed with a special orchid fertilizer during the flowering period. Do not feed during the remainder of the year.

Special care: Repot in early spring only if the roots need more space, using orchid compost.

Pests and diseases: Spider mites and fungus disease.

Other species/cultivars: There are many cultivars, offering a wide range of different flower colors.

Propagation: In spring, divide the plant or remove the back bulb.

plant type	light	draft tolerant	water		feeding	flowering season	lowest temperature
		✕	✕	spring			
				summer	✕	✕	50°F (10°C)
				fall			
				winter			

Cyperus diffusus

Dwarf Umbrella Grass/Diffused Flatsedge

Family: *Cyperaceae*

Use: A sculptural marsh plant for indoors, or a greenhouse or sunroom in summer.

Origin: Tropical South Africa.

Plant description: Compact, bushy perennial plant with a short rhizome and three-angled stems with crowns of broad, matte, green leaves and long, pale brown spikelets.

Light and position: Filtered sunlight. Keep the plant away from full sun.

Temperature range: Warm to cool, tolerating temperatures down to 50°F (10°C).

Water: This marsh plant must be kept constantly moist, so water freely at all times. It can tolerate standing in water.

Feeding: Feed with a low-nitrogen fertilizer once a month from spring to fall. Do not feed during the remainder of the year.

Special care: Repot every year in spring. Cut away any yellow stems.

Pests and diseases: Spider mites.

Other species/cultivars: *C. alternifolia* 'Zumula' has slender stems bearing a crown of long, grass-like leaves. *C. involucratus* has ribbed stems with a crown of grass-like leaves around a head of small, brown flowers.

Propagation: Cuttings should be taken from a mature stem, ¾ in (2 cm) below the rosette. Remove the tops of the bracts before potting.

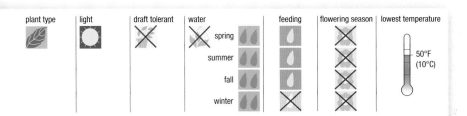

plant type	light	draft tolerant	water		feeding	flowering season	lowest temperature
			spring				50°F (10°C)
			summer				
			fall				
			winter				

plant type

light

draft tolerant

water

feeding

flowering season

lowest temperature

50°F
(10°C)

Dendrobium
Orchid (hybrids)

Family: *Orchidaceae*

Use: Flowering orchid for indoors, or a greenhouse or sunroom in summer.

Plant description: Epiphytic orchid with elongated pseudobulbs (thickened bulb-like stems) and long leaves. The white or purple flowers are clustered in arching racemes.

Light and position: Filtered sun. Keep the plant away from full sun.

Temperature range: Warm to cool, tolerating temperatures down to 50°F (10°C).

Water: Water regularly with soft water from spring to fall and avoid letting the soil dry out. Water more sparingly during winter.

Feeding: Feed with an orchid fertilizer once a month during the flowering period. Do not feed during the remainder of the year.

Special care: This plant prefers a rest period during winter, when it should be kept in a light, dry, and cool position, at about 59°F (15°C). Repot every second or third year in early spring, using orchid compost.

Pests and diseases: Scale insects, spider mites, and fungus disease.

Other species/cultivars: There are more than a hundred species and hybrids.

Propagation: Repot the plantlets or take stem cuttings in spring.

Dieffenbachia maculata

Dumb Cane/Mother-in-
Law Plant/Leopard's Lily

Family: *Araceae*

Use: Foliage ornamental for indoors, or a greenhouse or sunroom in summer.

Origin: Tropical South America.

Plant description: Tough, herbaceous plant with an erect, fleshy stem and large leaves highly variegated with white, yellow, or yellow-green.

Light and position: Filtered sun; avoid full sun. Direct sunlight will result in paler leaf colors.

Temperature range: Prefers a warm position but tolerates temperatures down to 41°F (5°C).

Water: Water regularly with soft water, allowing the soil to dry out slightly before watering again. The plant also enjoys a monthly shower in the bathroom.

Feeding: Feed with a low-nitrogen fertilizer once a month from spring to fall. Do not feed during the remainder of the year.

Special care: This is a poisonous plant that should be kept out of the reach of children. It will stop growing and start flowering if kept below 59°F (15°C) for two to three months. Cut back in early spring to promote more compact new growth. Repot every second year in early spring.

Pests and diseases: Aphids, mealy bugs, scale insects, spider mites, and gray mold.

Other species/ cultivars: There are many cultivars, mainly varying in plant size and in leaf color and variegation.

Propagation: In spring, take cuttings from stem tips or basal sideshoots.

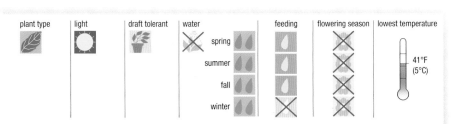

plant type	light	draft tolerant	water			feeding	flowering season	lowest temperature
			spring					
			summer					41°F (5°C)
			fall					
			winter					

Dracaena marginata
Madagascar Dragon Tree/
Dragon Tree/Ribbon Plant

Family: *Dracaenaceae*

Use: Sculptural foliage tree for indoors, or a greenhouse or sunroom in summer.

Origin: Reunion Island.

Plant description: Tough shrub with a slender trunk terminating in rosettes of narrow, elongated, lance-shaped leaves, colored olive-green with red margins.

Light and position: Full to filtered sun.

Temperature range: Warm to cool, tolerating temperatures down to 46°F (8°C).

Water: Water regularly, allowing the soil to dry out slightly before watering again.

Feeding: Feed with a low-nitrogen fertilizer every two weeks from spring to fall. Do not feed during the remainder of the year.

Special care: Repot the plant every second or third year in early spring. Long shoots can be cut back at the same time to promote bushy new growth.

Pests and diseases: Aphids, mealy bugs, scale insects, and spider mites.

Other species/cultivars: There are many cultivars and species of *Dracaena*. The cultivar 'Bicolor' has cream-striped leaves with pink margins. *D. fragrans* forms woody trunks and has broader leaves with stripes in a wide range of different shades of green. *D. sanderiana* has narrow, elongated, twisted leaves, colored grass green with marginal bands of white.

Propagation: Stem cuttings can be taken at any time of year.

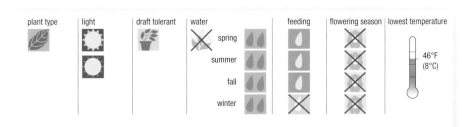

plant type	light	draft tolerant	water		feeding	flowering season	lowest temperature
			spring				
			summer				46°F (8°C)
			fall				
			winter				

Echinocactus grusonii
Golden Barrel Cactus/Mother-in-law's
Seat/Mother-in-law's Cushion

Family: *Cactaceae*

Use: Sculptural cactus for indoors, or a greenhouse or sunroom in summer.

Origin: Mexico.

Plant description: Large cactus that is globular in form when young and barrel-shaped later. It is closely ribbed and covered with bright golden spines and bears small, funnel-shaped, yellow flowers in summer.

Light and position: Full sun, tolerating filtered sun for a short time.

Temperature range: Warm to cool, tolerating temperatures down to 50°F (10°C). Cooler during winter.

Water: This plant will rot and die if overwatered. Water regularly from spring to summer, allowing the soil to dry out before watering again. Keep the soil almost dry during winter, especially if the plant is kept cool.

Feeding: Feed with a low-nitrogen fertilizer once a month from spring to summer. Do not feed during the remainder of the year.

Special care: The plant prefers a dormant period during winter, when it should be kept in a light, cool position at 50–59°F (10–15°C). Repot every second or third year in early spring.

Pests and diseases: Mealy bugs and scale insects.

Other species/cultivars: None.

Propagation: Seeds can be sown from spring to fall.

plant type

light

draft tolerant

water

spring summer fall winter

feeding

flowering season

lowest temperature

50°F
(10°C)

Epipremnum pinnatum
Tongavine

Family: *Araceae*

Use: Foliage climber for indoors, or a greenhouse or sunroom in summer.

Origin: Malaysia, New Guinea, and Pacific Islands.

Plant description: Tough climber with leaves that change shape as the plant matures. When the leaves are young, they are entire and oblique-ovate; when mature, they are oblong and pinnately parted. The leaves are colored shiny grass-green, blotched with yellow or white.

Light and position: Filtered sun. Keep the plant away from full sun.

Temperature range: Warm to cool, tolerating temperatures down to 59°F (15°C).

Water: Water regularly, allowing the soil to dry out slightly before watering again. Mist the plant frequently with a hand-spray to maintain high humidity.

Feeding: Feed with a low-nitrogen fertilizer once a month from spring to summer. Do not feed during the remainder of the year.

Special care: This plant prefers high humidity. It can be cut back at any time of year to promote more compact new growth. Repot every second year in spring.

Pests and diseases: Mealy bugs, scale insects, spider mites, and gray mold.

Other species/cultivars: The cultivar 'Areum' has yellow-blotched leaves. 'Marble Queen' has white-blotched leaves.

Propagation: Stem or stem-tip cuttings from softwood or semi-ripe shoots can be taken all year round. The cuttings should be placed in a heated propagator or on a propagation blanket, with a bottom heat of 70–77°F (21–25°C).

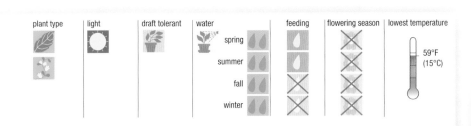

plant type	light	draft tolerant	water		feeding	flowering season	lowest temperature
				spring			59°F (15°C)
				summer			
				fall			
				winter			

Euphorbia milii
Crown of Thorns/Christ Thorn

Family: *Euphorbiaceae*

Use: Flowering, sculptural shrub for indoors, or a greenhouse or sunroom in summer.

Origin: Madagascar.

Plant description: Tough, branching, spiny shrub with deciduous, obovate leaves, light green in color. Its inflorescence displays bicolored, petal-like bracts sheltering small, yellow flowers. The plant produces a white sap.

Light and position: Prefers full sunlight; tolerates filtered sun.

Temperature range: Warm to cool, tolerating temperatures down to 41°F (5°C). Cooler during winter.

Water: Water regularly, allowing the soil to dry out before watering again. Keep the soil drier if the plant is kept cool during winter.

The plant tolerates drying out for about a month; this will promote flowering.

Feeding: Feed with a low-nitrogen fertilizer once a month from spring to fall. Do not feed during the remainder of the year.

Special care: Use gloves when handling this plant as its sap irritates the skin. The plant prefers a dormant period during winter, when it should be kept in a light, cool position at 41–50°F (5–10°C). Repot every second year in early spring. At the same time, long shoots can be cut back to promote more compact new growth.

Pests and diseases: Mealy bugs, scale insects, spider mites, and gray mold.

Other species/cultivars: Many cultivars exist, varying in plant size and bract color, which may be white, cream, salmon, light red, or dark red. 'Vulcanus' is larger in plant and leaf size and has bigger, dull red bracts.

Propagation: Stem cuttings can be taken in late spring.

plant type

light

draft tolerant

water

spring	summer	fall	winter

feeding

flowering season

lowest temperature

41°F
(5°C)

Euphorbia pulcherrima
Christmas Star/
Mexican Flame Leaf/Lobster Plant/
Poinsettia/Painted Leaf/Christmas Flower

Family: *Euphorbiaceae*

Use: Flowering ornamental shrub for indoors, especially at Christmas.
Origin: South Mexico and Central America.
Plant description: Branching shrub with ovate, dark green leaves and showy lance-shaped bracts surrounding small, yellow flowers. The bracts may be white, salmon, light red, dark red, or purple. The plant produces a white sap.
Light and position: Prefers filtered sunlight; tolerates full sun.
Temperature range: Warm to cool, tolerating temperatures down to 41°F (5°C).
Water: Keep the soil constantly moist, as the plant does not tolerate drying out. Water by standing the pot in water for ten minutes.
Feeding: None.
Special care: Protect the plant against cold, as this may result in leaf drop. The sap may cause irritation; avoid contact with skin or eyes. Discard the plant after flowering.
Pests and diseases: Mealy bugs, scale insects, spider mites, white fly, and gray mold.

Other species/cultivars: There are many cultivars, varying in bract color and form.
Propagation: Top cuttings can be taken from spring to summer, but producing flowering plants is difficult.

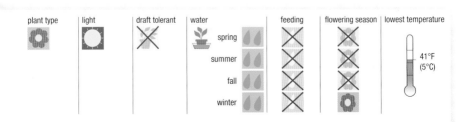

plant type	light	draft tolerant	water		feeding	flowering season	lowest temperature
				spring			
				summer			41°F (5°C)
				fall			
				winter			

Euphorbia tirucalli

Pencil Tree/Milkbush/Rubber
Euphorbia/Finger Tree/Tiru-Malu

Family: *Euphorbiaceae*

Use: Sculptural shrub for indoors, or a greenhouse or sunroom in summer.

Origin: East Africa, South Africa, and Madagascar.

Plant description: Tough, spineless shrub or tree with pencil-like, dark green branches and a few small, grass-green leaves at the tips of growing branches. The flowers are also found clustered at the apexes of the branches. The plant produces a milky sap.

Light and position: Prefers full sunlight; tolerates filtered sun.

Temperature range: Warm to cool, tolerating temperatures down to 41°F (5°C). Prefers a cool position during winter.

Water: Water regularly during growing season, allowing the soil to dry out slightly before watering again. Keep the soil almost dry during the rest of the year. The plant tolerates drying out for one month.

Feeding: Feed with a low-nitrogen fertilizer once a month from spring to fall. Do not feed during the remainder of the year.

Special care: The milky sap causes irritation; avoid contact with skin or eyes. The plant prefers a dormant period during winter, when it should be kept in a light, cool position at 41–50°F (5–10°C). Repot every second year in early spring.

Pests and diseases: Aphids, mildew, and gray mold.

Other species/cultivars: None.

Propagation: Branch cuttings can be taken from spring to summer.

plant type

light

draft tolerant

water

spring   summer   fall   winter

feeding

flowering season

lowest temperature

41°F
(5°C)

Euphorbia trigona
African Milk Plant/Spurge

Family: *Euphorbiaceae*

Use: Tough, sculptural succulent for indoors, a greenhouse, or a sunroom.

Origin: Namibia.

Plant description: Succulent candelabra, ranging in size from shrub to small tree. The three-angled stems have closely toothed ridges and a milky sap, and bear deciduous, oval leaves.

Light and position: Full sunlight to filtered sun.

Temperature range: Warm, cooler during winter. Tolerates temperatures down to 41°F (5°C).

Water: This plant will die if overwatered. Water regularly from spring to fall, allowing the soil to dry out before watering again. The soil should be almost dry during winter if the plant is kept cool. Tolerates dry air.

Feeding: Feed with a low-nitrogen fertilizer once a month from spring to fall. Do not feed during the remainder of the year.

Special care: The milky sap may cause irritation; avoid contact with skin or eyes. The plant requires good drainage. It prefers a dormant period during winter, when it should be kept in a light, cool position at about 50–59°F (10–15°C). Repot every second or third year in early spring.

Pests and diseases: Mealy bugs, scale insects, spider mites, white fly, and mildew.

Other species/cultivars: Many species are cultivated. *E. milli* has thorny branches and long flower stalks with red, white, or orange bracts. *E. pugniformis* trails cylindrical, tuber-like branches. The cylindrical branches of *E. tirucalli* are the thickness of a pencil and grow upright.

Propagation: Take long stem cuttings in late spring.

plant type	light	draft tolerant	water		feeding	flowering season	lowest temperature
			spring				
			summer				41°F (5°C)
			fall				
			winter				

Exacum affine
German Violet/Persian Violet

Family: *Gentianaceae*

Use: Flowering plant for indoors, a greenhouse or sunroom, or a sheltered spot outdoors.

Origin: Socotra (Yemen).

Plant description: Compact, herbaceous plant with stalked, oval leaves and an abundance of fragrant flowers, shaped like stars. The flowers may be single or double and are colored white, blue, or purple, with an eye of deep yellow stamens.

Light and position: Full sunlight to filtered sun.

Temperature range: Warm to cool, tolerating temperatures down to 41°F (5°C).

Water: Water regularly all year round, allowing the soil to dry out before watering again. Do not water the soil directly, but stand the pot in water for ten minutes. The plant will rot and die if overwatered.

Feeding: None.

Special care: The plant will flower only if exposed to sufficient light, and should be discarded after flowering.

Pests and diseases: Aphids, mealy bugs, and spider mites.

Other species/cultivars: There is a range of cultivars, offering different flower colors.

Propagation: Seeds are sown in spring.

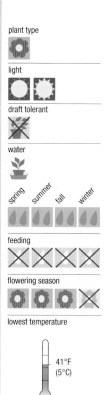

plant type

light

draft tolerant

water

spring summer fall winter

feeding

flowering season

lowest temperature

41°F
(5°C)

plant type

light

draft tolerant

water

spring summer fall winter

feeding

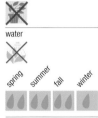

flowering season

lowest temperature

41°F
(5°C)

Fatsia japonica
Japanese Fatsia

Family: *Araliaceae*

Use: A sculptural foliage plant for indoors, a greenhouse or sunroom, or outdoors in summer.

Origin: Japan, Riukiu Islands, Cambodia, and South Korea.

Plant description: Evergreen shrub with glossy, lobed leaves, colored dark green, and milky white flowers.

Light and position: Filtered sunlight to shade. Keep the plant away from direct sunlight.

Temperature range: Warm, cooler during winter. Tolerates temperatures down to 41°F (5°C).

Water: Water regularly from spring to fall, allowing the soil to dry out slightly before watering again. Water more sparingly during the rest of the year.

Feeding: Feed with a low-nitrogen fertilizer every two weeks from spring to fall. Do not feed during the remainder of the year.

Special care: The plant prefers a dormant period during winter, when it should be kept in a light, cool position at about 41–50°F (5–10°C). Repot every year in early spring.

Pests and diseases: Aphids, scale insects, spider mites, and gray mold.

Other species/cultivars: The leaves of *F. japonica* 'Variegata' are variegated green and cream-white.

Propagation: Seeds are sown in spring, and stem cuttings from semi-ripe shoots may be taken at any time of year.

Ficus benjamina
Tropic Laurel/Weeping Fig/Benjamin Tree/
Java Tree/Small-Leaved Rubber Plant

Family: *Moraceae*

Use: Tough, sculptural, foliage plant for indoors, or a greenhouse or sunroom in summer.

Origin: The Himalayas, India, Myanmar, South China, Malay Archipelago, and North Australia.

Plant description: Tall tree with a mass of drooping branches and shiny, elongated, oval leaves, colored dark green.

Light and position: Full to filtered sun. Too little light will result in leaf drop.

Temperature range: Warm to cool, tolerating temperatures down to 32°F (0°C).

Water: Water well from spring to fall, more sparingly during the rest of the year. The plant tolerates dry air.

Feeding: Feed with a low-nitrogen fertilizer every two weeks from spring to fall. Do not feed during the remainder of the year.

Special care: Overwatering, overfertilizing, or too shady a site will cause the leaves to drop. The plant should be placed in a light position during winter. Repot every second or third year in spring.

Pests and diseases: Mealy bugs, scale insects, and gray mold.

Other species/cultivars: Many cultivars are grown, offering a variety of leaf sizes and colors ranging from dark green to yellow and white splashed with green. Some cultivars are tall; others are small and compact. Some produce small fruits, blood-red when ripe, which are not edible.

Propagation: Take stem cuttings from greenwood to semi-ripe shoots at any time of year. The cuttings should be placed in a heated propagator or on a propagation blanket, with a bottom heat of 68–77°F (20–25°C).

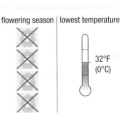

plant type	light	draft tolerant	water		feeding	flowering season	lowest temperature
			spring				
			summer				32°F (0°C)
			fall				
			winter				

Saber Ficus/Narrow-Leaf Fig

Family: *Moraceae*

Use: Tough, sculptural, foliage plant for indoors, or a greenhouse or sunroom in summer.

Origin: Malay Archipelago.

Plant description: Elegant tree with a mass of drooping branches and shiny, lance-shaped leaves.

Light and position: Full to filtered sun. Too little light will result in leaf drop.

Temperature range: Warm to cool, tolerating temperatures down to 32°F (0°C).

Water: Water well from spring to fall, more sparingly during the remainder of the year. The plant tolerates dry air.

Feeding: Feed with a low-nitrogen fertilizer every two weeks from spring to fall. Do not feed during the rest of the year.

Special care: Overwatering, overfertilizing, or too shady a site will cause the leaves to drop. Place the plant in a light position during winter. Repot every second or third year in spring.

Pests and diseases: Mealy bugs, scale insects, and gray mold.

Other species/cultivars: None.

Propagation: Take stem cuttings from greenwood to semi-ripe shoots at any time of year. The cuttings should be placed in a heated propagator or on a propagation blanket, with a bottom heat of 68–77°F (20–25°C).

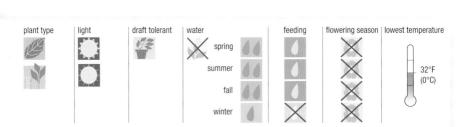

plant type	light	draft tolerant	water		feeding	flowering season	lowest temperature
			spring				
			summer				32°F (0°C)
			fall				
			winter				

Ficus deltoidea

Mistletoe Fig/Mistletoe Rubber Plant

Family: *Moraceae*

Use: A sculptural, foliage plant for indoors, or a greenhouse or sunroom in summer.

Origin: Malay Archipelago.

Plant description: Very tough, woody shrub with stiff, dark green leaves. It bears small, round, yellowish figs, which are not edible.

Light and position: Full sunlight to filtered sun.

Temperature range: Warm to cool, tolerating temperatures down to 32°F (0°C).

Water: Water regularly from spring to fall, allowing the soil to dry out slightly before watering again. Water more sparingly during the rest of the year.

Feeding: Feed with a low-nitrogen fertilizer every two weeks from spring to fall. Do not feed during the remainder of the year.

Special care: Repot every second or third year in spring.

Pests and diseases: Mealy bugs, scale insects, and gray mold.

Other species/cultivars: None.

Propagation: Take stem cuttings from greenwood to semi-ripe shoots at any time of year. The cuttings should be placed in a heated propagator or on a propagation blanket, with a bottom heat of 68–77°F (20–25°C).

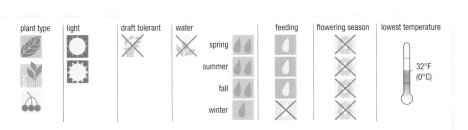

plant type	light	draft tolerant	water		feeding	flowering season	lowest temperature
			spring				
			summer				32°F (0°C)
			fall				
			winter				

Ficus lyrata
Fiddle Leaf Fig/Banjo Fig

Family: *Moraceae*

Use: A sculptural, foliage plant for indoors, or a greenhouse or sunroom in summer.

Origin: West Africa.

Plant description: Tree with large, thick, violin-shaped leaves, which have a leathery texture and yellow-green veins.

Light and position: Full sunlight to filtered sun.

Temperature range: Warm to cool, tolerating temperatures down to 32°F (0°C).

Water: Water regularly from spring to fall, allowing the soil to dry out slightly before watering again. Water more sparingly during the rest of the year. This plant benefits from regular misting with a hand-spray.

Feeding: Feed with a low-nitrogen fertilizer every two weeks from spring to fall. Do not feed during the remainder of the year.

Special care: Repot every second or third year in spring.

Pests and diseases: Mealy bugs, scale insects, and gray mold.

Other species/cultivars: *F. lyrata* 'Bambino' is smaller in plant height and size of leaves. *F. elatica* has large, oblong, glossy leaves, leathery in texture, which when young are enclosed in a reddish sheath.

Propagation: Take stem cuttings from greenwood to semi-ripe shoots at any time of year. The cuttings should be placed in a heated propagator or on a propagation blanket, with a bottom heat of 68–77°F (20–25°C).

plant type	light	draft tolerant	water		feeding	flowering season	lowest temperature
			spring				
			summer				32°F (0°C)
			fall				
			winter				

Fortunella japonica
Round Kumquat/
Marumi Kumquat

Family: *Rutaceae*

Use: Small fruit tree for indoors, a greenhouse or sunroom, or outdoors in summer. The fruit may be grown for culinary use.

Origin: South China.

Plant description: Small, spiny fruit tree with lance-shaped, light green leaves and fragrant, white flowers. It bears small, egg-shaped fruit which may be eaten.

Light and position: Full sunlight to filtered sun.

Temperature range: Warm, cooler during winter. Tolerates temperatures down to 32°F (0°C).

Water: Water from spring to fall, allowing the soil to dry out slightly before watering again. Keep the soil almost dry in winter.

Feeding: Feed with a low-nitrogen fertilizer every two weeks from spring to fall. Do not feed during the remainder of the year.

Special care: The tree requires good drainage. It also needs a rest period from October to April, when it should be kept in a light, cool position, at about 41°F (5°C). Repot every year in spring.

Pests and diseases: Spider mites.

Other species/cultivars: The cultivar 'Fucushii' bears large, oval, edible fruit. The small, oblong, bright orange fruit of *F. margarita* are also edible.

Propagation: Take stem cuttings from semi-ripe shoots in summer. The cuttings should be placed in a heated propagator or on a propagation blanket, with a bottom heat of 68–77°F (20–25°C).

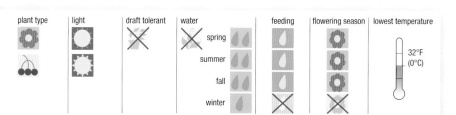

plant type	light	draft tolerant	water		feeding	flowering season	lowest temperature
			spring				
			summer				32°F (0°C)
			fall				
			winter				

Fuchsia/Lady's Eardrops (hybrids)

Family: *Onagraceae*

Use: Flowering ornamental plant for indoors, a greenhouse or sunroom, or outdoors from spring to fall. Some pendant cultivars are ideal for hanging baskets.

Plant description: Vigorous shrub with dark green, ovate leaves and pendant, tubular flowers clustered in terminal racemes. The flowers come in a wide range of shapes and colors, from white to cream, salmon, orange, pink, cerise, or purple.

Light and position: Filtered sunlight. Keep the plant away from full sun.

Temperature range: Prefers a cool position, tolerating temperatures down to 41°F (5°C).

Water: Keep the soil constantly moist from spring to fall. Water very sparingly when dormant during winter, but never allow the plant to dry out.

Feeding: Feed with a low-nitrogen fertilizer every two weeks from spring to fall. Do not feed during the remainder of the year.

Special care: This plant prefers a dormant period during winter, when it should be kept in a light, cool position, at 41–50°F (5–10°C). Cut the plant back and repot it in early spring, using a small container.

Pests and diseases: Aphids, mealy bugs, white fly, and gray mold.

Other species/cultivars: There are a great many cultivars, varying in plant size and in the shape and color of the flowers.

Propagation: Stem cuttings may be taken from softwood at any time of year. Cuttings of semi-ripe shoots can be taken from summer to fall.

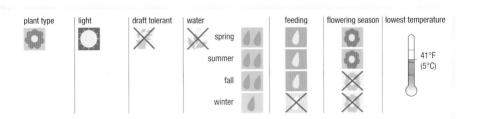

plant type	light	draft tolerant	water		feeding	flowering season	lowest temperature
			spring				
			summer				41°F (5°C)
			fall				
			winter				

Gardenia augusta
Cape Jasmine/Gardenia/Jasmin
Family: *Rubiaceae*

Use: Flowering shrub for indoors, or a greenhouse or sunroom in summer.

Origin: Japan, Riukiu Islands, Taiwan, and China.

Plant description: Evergreen shrub with glossy, dark green leaves and beautifully scented, double, white flowers.

Light and position: Filtered sunlight; keep the plant away from full sun.

Temperature range: Warm, cooler during winter. Tolerates temperatures down to 59°F (15°C).

Water: Water regularly with soft water from spring to fall, more sparingly during the rest of the year. Avoid letting the soil dry out, which will result in yellow flower buds.

Feeding: Feed with an acid fertilizer every two weeks from spring to fall. Do not feed during the remainder of the year.

Special care: The shrub may be cut back, but no later than August or the formation of flower buds will be disturbed. Allow the plant a dormant period during winter, keeping it in a light, cool position, at about 59–64°F (15–18°C). Repot in ericaceous (lime-free) potting soil every year in spring.

Pests and diseases: Aphids, scale insects, and gray mold.

Other species/cultivars: The cultivar 'Veitchii' is the most commonly used, chosen for its compact bushy growth.

Propagation: Greenwood and semi-ripe stem-tip cuttings may be taken at any time of year. The cuttings should be placed in a heated propagator or on a propagation blanket, with a bottom heat of 68–77°F (20–25°C).

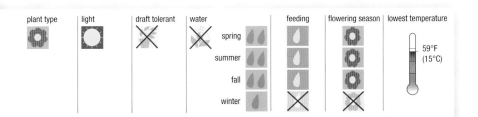

plant type	light	draft tolerant	water		feeding	flowering season	lowest temperature
				spring			
				summer			59°F (15°C)
				fall			
				winter			

Gerbera jamesonii
Barberton Daisy/Gerbera/
Transvaal Daisy

Family: *Asteraceae*

Use: Flowering plant for indoors, a greenhouse or sunroom, or outdoors in summer.

Origin: South Africa.

Plant description: Compact, herbaceous perennial with large, lobed leaves, hairy in texture. The long-lasting, daisy-like flowers may be single or double and are found in a broad range of colors, such as white, yellow, orange, pink, or red.

Light and position: Full sunlight to filtered sun.

Temperature range: Warm to cool, tolerating temperatures down to 41°F (5°C).

Water: Water regularly from spring to fall, allowing the soil to dry out before watering again. Water more sparingly during the rest of the year.

Feeding: Feed with a low-nitrogen fertilizer once a month from spring to fall. Do not feed during the remainder of the year.

Special care: Discard the plant after flowering when there are no more flower buds.

Pests and diseases: Aphids, spider mites, white fly, and gray mold.

Other species/cultivars: There is a wide range of cultivars available, offering a variety of sizes and flower colors.

Propagation: Seeds are sown in spring.

plant type

light

draft tolerant

water

spring summer fall winter

feeding

flowering season

lowest temperature

41°F
(5°C)

plant type

light

draft tolerant

water

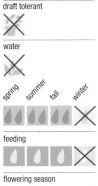

spring summer fall winter

feeding

flowering season

lowest temperature

41°F
(5°C)

Gloriosa superba
Glory Lily/Flamelily/
Creeping Lily/Climbing Lily

Family: *Colchicaceae*

Use: Flowering climber for indoors, a greenhouse or sunroom, or outdoors in summer.

Origin: Tropical Africa and tropical Asia.

Plant description: Summer-growing, perennial climber with tuberous roots and tendril-like leaves. The flowers are beautiful, with their red and yellow petals bent back and stamens arching outward.

Light and position: Prefers full sunlight; tolerates filtered sun.

Temperature range: Warm to cool, tolerating temperatures down to 41°F (5°C) during the dormant period.

Water: Water regularly in growing season, allowing the soil to dry out before watering again. Do not water during the dormant period.

Feeding: Feed with a low-nitrogen fertilizer once a month from spring to the onset of the rest period in fall.

Special care: After flowering, when the leaves start to yellow, stop watering and let the plant wither. During winter, keep the roots in their pot and make sure they remain dry. Repot the roots in early spring, placing them at a temperature of 41–68°F (5–20°C), and start watering again. Take care when handling the tubers, as they can irritate the skin. Avoid harming the bulb.

Pests and diseases: Spider mites.

Other species/cultivars: The cultivar 'Rothschildiana' has striped flowers with wavy margins.

Propagation: In spring, from seeds or by division of the finger-like tubers that are formed.

plant type

light

draft tolerant

water

spring summer fall winter

feeding

flowering season

lowest temperature

59°F
(15°C)

Guzmania dissitiflora

Guzmania

Family: *Bromeliaceae*

Use: Flowering bromeliad for indoors, or a greenhouse or sunroom in summer.
Origin: Costa Rica, Panama, and Colombia.
Plant description: Tough epiphyte with a rosette of soft, linear leaves in light green and an erect inflorescence of bright red and yellow bracts.

Light and position: The plant tolerates a broad spectrum of light, but keep it away from full sun.
Temperature range: Warm, tolerating temperatures down to 59°F (15°C).
Water: Water with lukewarm water inside the rosette. The plant tolerates drying out for a few weeks.
Feeding: Feed inside the rosette with a low-nitrogen fertilizer once a month from spring to fall. Do not feed during the remainder of the year.
Special care: Water and fertilize inside the rosette, which should always contain water except when the plant is kept at a low temperature. Repot offsets in spring.
Pests and diseases: Mealy bugs.
Other species/cultivars: Many species and cultivars are grown, varying in color and shape of inflorescence and leaf.
Propagation: Divide the offsets in spring.

Hedera helix

Common Ivy/English Ivy

Family: *Araliaceae*

Use: Foliage climber for indoors, a greenhouse or sunroom, or outdoors. Ideal for a trellis, hoop, or hanging basket.

Origin: Europe.

Plant description: Climbing vine with five-lobed, dark green leaves displaying creamy veins.

Light and position: Filtered sunlight; keep the plant away from full sun from spring to fall.

Temperature range: Warm to cool temperatures. Frost hardy in the garden.

Water: This plant will rot and die if overwatered. Water regularly in growing season, allowing the soil to dry out before watering again, and more sparingly during the rest of the year.

Feeding: Feed with a low-nitrogen fertilizer every two weeks from spring to fall. Do not feed during the remainder of the year.

Special care: Needs support and therefore suitable for training to a hoop or small trellis, or for growing in a hanging basket. Long shoots can be cut back to promote more bushy growth. Repot every year in spring.

Pests and diseases: Aphids, mealy bugs, scale insects, spider mites, and gray mold.

Other species/cultivars: The species *H. canariensis* have larger leaves. Many cultivars are available, offering different leaf shapes and sizes, and variegation ranging from white and yellow to mint green.

Propagation: Stem cuttings from softwood may be taken at any time of year.

plant type

light

draft tolerant

water

spring   summer   fall   winter

feeding

flowering season

lowest temperature

5°F
(-15°C)

China Hibiscus/
Rose of China/Hawaiian Hibiscus/Shoe Black

Family: *Malvaceae*

Use: Flowering shrub for indoors, a greenhouse or sunroom, or outdoors in summer.

Origin: Tropical Asia.

Plant description: Tough, evergreen shrub or small tree with large, glossy, dark green leaves. The solitary flowers, which may be single or double, are large and showy, in a broad range of bright colors such as white, yellow, rose, orange, red, or lavender.

Light and position: Prefers full sunlight; tolerates filtered sun.

Temperature range: Warm to cool, tolerating temperatures down to 54°F (12°C).

Water: Water plentifully from spring to fall, more sparingly during winter. The plant tolerates a slight drying out.

Feeding: Feed with a low-nitrogen fertilizer every two weeks from spring to fall. Do not feed during the remainder of the year.

Special care: In fall, after flowering, the shoots can be cut back, and the plant should be repotted at the same time. Some of the leaves may drop during winter, but the plant will regenerate in spring.

Pests and diseases: Aphids, mealy bugs, scale insects, spider mites, gray mold, and white fly.

Other species/cultivars: Many cultivars are grown, varying in flower color.

Propagation: Stem cuttings from softwood or from semi-ripe shoots may be taken from early to late summer.

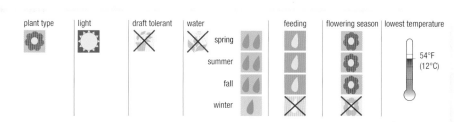

plant type	light	draft tolerant	water		feeding	flowering season	lowest temperature
			spring				
			summer				54°F (12°C)
			fall				
			winter				

Amaryllis/Knight's Star Lily (hybrids)

Family: *Amaryllidaceae*

Use: Flowering bulb for indoors, a greenhouse, or a sunroom.

Plant description: The plant forms a round bulb and a tall stem tipped with large flowers, which may be white, cream, red, or bicolored. The flowers appear before the leaves, which are shiny, long, and strap-like.

Light and position: Prefers full sunlight; tolerates filtered sun.

Temperature range: Warm to cool, tolerating temperatures down to 41°F (5°C).

Water: Water sparingly before and during flowering. When the leaves appear, water regularly, allowing the soil to dry out slightly before watering again. Do not water in the dormant period.

Feeding: Feed with a low-nitrogen fertilizer every two weeks during growing season, from after flowering until the rest period begins.

Special care: The plant needs a dormant period. Stop watering the plant in late summer and place it in a cooler position, at about 50–59°F (10–15°C), which will make the leaves wither. After a few months, it will be possible to make the bulb flower again. Repot the bulb, place it in a warmer position, and start watering again.

Pests and diseases: None.

Other species/cultivars: A range of cultivars display a variety of flower colors.

Propagation: Divide large offsets from the parent bulb in late winter or early spring.

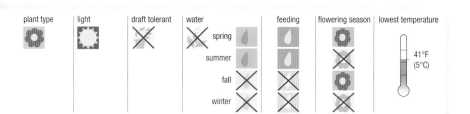

plant type	light	draft tolerant	water		feeding	flowering season	lowest temperature
			spring				
			summer				41°F (5°C)
			fall				
			winter				

Howea forsteriana

Kentia Palm/Paradise Palm/
Sentry Palm/Thatch Leaf Palm/
Forster Sentry Palm

Family: *Arecaceae*

Use: A sculptural palm for indoors, or a greenhouse or sunroom in summer.

Origin: Lord Howe Islands.

Plant description: Tough palm with pinnate, grass-green leaves, which grow larger on slender stems.

Light and position: Filtered sunlight; keep the plant away from full sun.

Temperature range: Warm to cool, tolerating temperatures down to 50°F (10°C).

Water: Keep the soil constantly moist, especially during growing season. The plant does not tolerate drying out. Mist frequently with a hand-spray to maintain high humidity.

Feeding: Feed with a low-nitrogen fertilizer once a month from spring to fall. Do not feed during the remainder of the year.

Special care: The leaves will turn yellow if exposed to full sun. The plant should be repotted every third year in spring.

Pests and diseases: Mealy bugs, scale insects, and spider mites.

Other species/cultivars: None.

Propagation: Seeds are sown in spring.

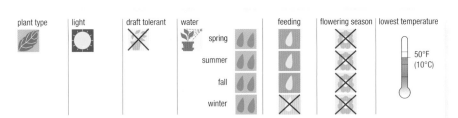

plant type	light	draft tolerant	water		feeding	flowering season	lowest temperature
				spring			
				summer			50°F (10°C)
				fall			
				winter			

plant type

light

draft tolerant

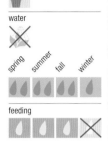

water

spring | summer | fall | winter

feeding

flowering season

lowest temperature

41°F
(5°C)

Hoya bella
Porcelain Flower/
Wax Flower

Family: *Asclepiadaceae*

Use: Flowering trailer for indoors, a greenhouse, or a sunroom; ideal for a hanging basket.

Origin: Myanmar.

Plant description: Shrubby plant with drooping branches and small, fleshy, oval leaves. The waxy, white flowers have purple hearts and hang clustered in pendent umbels.

Light and position: Filtered sunlight; keep the plant away from full sun.

Temperature range: Warm to cool, tolerating temperatures down to 41°F (5°C).

Water: Water regularly in growing season, allowing the soil to dry out before watering again. Keep the soil almost dry during the rest of the year.

Feeding: Feed with a low-nitrogen fertilizer once a month from spring to fall. Do not feed during the remainder of the year.

Special care: To form flower buds, this plant needs to receive more than twelve hours of light per day for at least a month. After flowering the plant may be cut back. It prefers a dormant period during winter, when it should be placed in a dry, cool position at about 59°F (15°C). It grows well in hanging baskets and should be repotted every second year in early spring.

Pests and diseases: Mealy bugs, scale insects, and spider mites.

Other species/cultivars: *H. linearis* has long branches with narrow, linear leaves.

Propagation: Tip cuttings may be taken in spring or summer.

plant type

light

draft tolerant

water

spring summer fall winter

feeding

flowering season

lowest temperature

5°F
(-15°C)

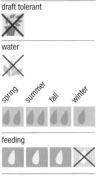

Hydrangea macrophylla
Hortensia/Lacecap Hydrangea

Family: *Hydrangeaceae*

Use: Flowering shrub for indoors, a greenhouse or sunroom, or outdoors.

Origin: Japan and Korea.

Plant description: Compact, freely branching shrub with large, sharply toothed, fresh-green leaves and medium to large clusters of white, blue, rose, or carmine flowers.

Light and position: Prefers filtered sunlight; tolerates full sun.

Temperature range: Warm to cool temperatures, lasting longer when placed in a cool position. Frost-hardy in the garden.

Water: Water plentifully during flowering and growing season, and avoid letting the soil dry out. Water more sparingly at other times of year.

Feeding: Feed with a low-nitrogen fertilizer every two weeks from spring to fall. Do not feed during the remainder of the year.

Special care: Discard after flowering, or plant in the garden.

Pests and diseases: Spider mites, gray mold, and mildew.

Other species/cultivars: There are many cultivars, offering a range of flower colors from white to rose, crimson, and blue.

Propagation: Take stem cuttings from softwood during late spring to midsummer, and from semi-ripe shoots in midsummer.

Jasminum polyanthum

Jasmine

Family: *Oleaceae*

Use: Flowering climber for indoors, a greenhouse or sunroom, or outdoors. Ideal for a small trellis.

Origin: West China.

Plant description: Climbing shrub with red branches and small, pinnate, dark green leaves, each with five to seven leaflets. A mass of deliciously scented, white flowers are produced from crimson buds.

Light and position: Prefers full sunlight; tolerates filtered sun.

Temperature range: Prefers a cool position, tolerating temperatures down to 32°F (0°C). Avoid placing the plant close to a radiator.

Water: Keep the soil constantly moist when the plant is flowering, and avoid drying out. Water more sparingly during the rest of the year.

Feeding: Feed with a low-nitrogen fertilizer every two weeks from spring to fall. Do not feed during the remainder of the year.

Special care: The flowers will last longer if the plant is placed in a light, cool position. Keep it in a cool place, such as the garden, during summer, as low temperatures will promote the formation of flower buds. Cut back the flowering branches after flowering. In fall, repot the plant and place it in a warmer position.

Pests and diseases: Aphids, spider mites, and gray mold.

Other species/cultivars: Many species are cultivated, a few as pot plants. *J. mesnyi* has long, arching branches and large, yellow flowers. *J. officinale* is a straggling bush with clusters of scented, white flowers.

Propagation: Stem cuttings from softwood or from semi-ripe shoots can be taken in spring and summer.

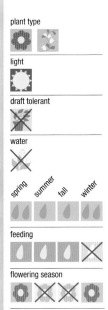

plant type

light

draft tolerant

water

spring summer fall winter

feeding

flowering season

lowest temperature

32°F
(0°C)

Juncus effusus 'Spiralis'
Corkscrew Rush/Spiral Rush/
Common Rush/Soft Rush

Family: *Juncaceae*

Use: Sculptural marsh plant for indoors, a greenhouse or sunroom, or outdoors.

Origin: North America, Europe, Asia, eastern and southern Africa.

Plant description: Rush with leaf-like, cylindrical stems that grow spirally, like a corkscrew. The leaves are plain green or green with lengthwise yellow stripes.

Light and position: Prefers full sunlight; tolerates filtered sun. Protect the plant from full sun during winter.

Temperature range: Prefers a cool position, and is frost-hardy in the garden.

Water: This marsh plant must be kept constantly moist, so water freely at all times. It tolerates standing in water.

Feeding: Feed with a low-nitrogen fertilizer once a month from spring to fall. Do not feed during the remainder of the year.

Special care: Protect the rush against direct sun if it is placed outdoors during winter. Repot every year in spring.

Pests and diseases: Aphids, mealy bugs, and gray mold.

Other species/cultivars: The leaf-like, cylindrical stems of *J. effusus* grow straight.

Propagation: The plant can be divided in early spring.

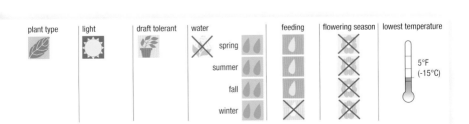

plant type	light	draft tolerant	water		feeding	flowering season	lowest temperature
			spring				
			summer				5°F (-15°C)
			fall				
			winter				

Justicia brandegeana
Shrimp Plant

Family: *Acanthaceae*

Use: Flowering shrub for indoors, a greenhouse or sunroom, or outdoors from spring to fall.

Origin: Northeast Mexico, naturalized in Florida.

Plant description: Small, compact shrub with hairy, ovate leaves. White flowers grow in pendant spikes under overlapping, reddish brown bracts.

Light and position: Prefers full sunlight; tolerates filtered sun.

Temperature range: Warm to cool, tolerating temperatures down to 41°F (5°C).

Water: Water regularly from spring to fall, allowing the soil to dry out slightly before watering again. Water more sparingly when the plant is kept cool in winter.

Feeding: Feed with a low-nitrogen fertilizer every two weeks from spring to fall. Do not feed during the remainder of the year.

Special care: To make the plant flower again, cut back and repot in fall. Place it in a light, cool position, at 50–59°F (10–15°C), and keep the soil dry. Put the plant in a warmer position and start watering again when new shoots and flower spikes appear in early spring.

Pests and diseases: Aphids, mealy bugs, spider mites, and gray mold.

Other species/cultivars: Other cultivars have yellow or yellow-green bracts.

Propagation: Stem cuttings can be taken in early spring. Place them in a heated propagator or on a propagation blanket, with a bottom heat of 68°F (20°C).

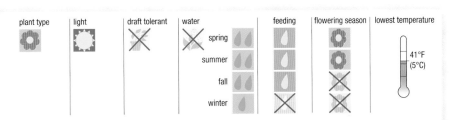

plant type	light	draft tolerant	water		feeding	flowering season	lowest temperature
				spring			
				summer			41°F (5°C)
				fall			
				winter			

Kalanchoe beharensis
Felt Bush/Felt Plant
Family: *Crassulaceae*

Use: A sculptural succulent for indoors, a greenhouse or sunroom, or outdoors in summer.

Origin: South Madagascar.

Plant description: Woody succulent with large, lobed leaves, shaped like arrows, and green-yellow flowers. The leaves have a hairy texture and are rust-colored on the top side and silver underneath.

Light and position: Full sunlight to filtered sun.

Temperature range: Warm to cool, tolerating temperatures down to 45°F (7°C).

Water: Water regularly from spring to fall, allowing the soil to dry out before watering again. Keep the soil almost dry in winter. The plant tolerates drying out for some time (about two to four weeks, depending on its position) but will rot and die if overwatered.

Feeding: Feed with a low-nitrogen fertilizer once a month from spring to fall. Do not feed during the remainder of the year.

Special care: This plant requires good drainage and during winter prefers to be kept dormant in a light, cool position, at about 50–59°F (10–15°C). It should be repotted every third year in early spring.

Pests and diseases: Aphids, mealy bugs, and gray mold.

Other species/cultivars: *K. thyrsifolia* has large, oval, hairy leaves, colored silvery light green with red at the tip and margins.

Propagation: New plants are formed at the base of mature leaves when these are removed from the plant and hung in a warm place, out of direct sunlight.

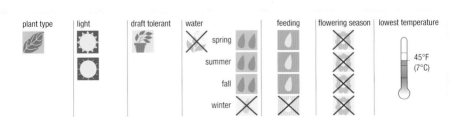

plant type	light	draft tolerant	water		feeding	flowering season	lowest temperature
			spring				
			summer				45°F (7°C)
			fall				
			winter				

plant type

light

draft tolerant

water

spring　summer　fall　winter

feeding

flowering season

lowest temperature

36°F
(2°C)

Kalanchoe blossfeldiana
Kalanchoe/Flaming Katy
Family: *Crassulaceae*

Use: Flowering plant for indoors, a greenhouse or sunroom, or outdoors in summer.

Origin: Madagascar.

Plant description: Compact plant with large, succulent, dark green leaves and dense clusters of upright, single or double flowers. The flowers are brightly colored in vivid shades of white *(right)*, cream *(left)*, yellow, orange, red *(below left)*, pink *(below right)*, or purple.

Light and position: Filtered sunlight to full sun. Exposing the plant to full sun during summer will redden its leaves.

Temperature range: Warm to cool, tolerating temperatures down to 36°F (2°C).

Water: Water regularly, allowing the soil to dry out before watering again. The plant tolerates drying out for some time (two to four weeks, depending on its position) but will rot and die if overwatered.

Feeding: Feed with a low-nitrogen fertilizer once a month from spring to fall. Do not feed during the remainder of the year.

Special care: The plant may flower again if it is placed under short-day conditions—that is, given less than eight hours of light per day—over a four-week period. Otherwise, discard after flowering.

Pests and diseases: Aphids, mealy bugs, and gray mold.

Other species/cultivars: Many cultivars, varying in flower color, are available. 'African' is larger in plant and flower size, with succulent, pinnate leaves. 'Mirabella' has small, succulent leaves and nodding, tubular flowers. 'Wendy' has larger, tubular, purple flowers.

Propagation: Stem cuttings can be taken from spring to fall.

Kalanchoe tomentosa

Panda Plant/Pussy Ears

Family: *Crassulaceae*

Use: A sculptural succulent for indoors, a greenhouse or sunroom, or outdoors in summer.

Origin: Central Madagascar.

Plant description: Succulent with erect, branching stems and fleshy, spoon-shaped leaves covered with white felt. The leaves have sharply toothed, brown margins.

Light and position: Full sunlight to filtered sun.

Temperature range: Warm to cool, tolerating temperatures down to 45°F (7°C).

Water: Water regularly from spring to fall, allowing the soil to dry out before watering again. Keep the soil almost dry in winter. The plant tolerates drying out for about a month, but will rot and die if overwatered.

Feeding: Feed with a low-nitrogen fertilizer once a month from spring to fall. Do not feed during the remainder of the year.

Special care: The plant needs good drainage and during winter prefers to be kept dormant in a light, cool position, at about 50–59°F (10–15°C). Repot every third year in early spring.

Pests and diseases. Aphids, mealy bugs, and gray mold.

Other species/cultivars: A broad range of species are cultivated.

Propagation: Stem cuttings can be taken from spring to fall.

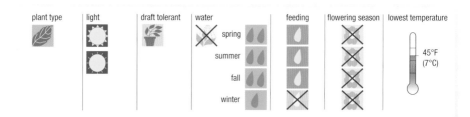

plant type	light	draft tolerant	water		feeding	flowering season	lowest temperature
				spring			
				summer			45°F (7°C)
				fall			
				winter			

Laurus nobilis

Bay Tree/Sweet Bay/ Grecian Laurel

Family: *Lauraceae*

Use: Small sculptural tree for indoors, a greenhouse or sunroom, or outdoors in summer. The leaves have a culinary use.

Origin: Europe.

Plant description: Small evergreen tree with aromatic, leathery, elliptic leaves used in cooking. The flowers are yellow-green, but insignificant.

Light and position: Prefers full sunlight; tolerates filtered sun.

Temperature range: Prefers a cool position, tolerating temperatures down to 41°F (5°C).

Water: Water plentifully from spring to fall, more sparingly during the rest of the year. The plant does not tolerate standing in water.

Feeding: Feed with a low-nitrogen fertilizer every two weeks from spring to fall. Do not feed during the remainder of the year.

Special care: This plant can be cut back (ideally during summer) and shaped as desired. It needs good drainage and prefers a dormant period during winter, when it should be kept in a light, cool position, at about 41–50°F (5–10°C). Repot every year in spring.

Pests and diseases: Mealy bugs and scale insects.

Other species/cultivars: None.

Propagation: Stem cuttings from semi-ripe shoots can be taken in late summer or early fall. Place the potted cuttings in a plastic bag to create the high humidity required for rooting.

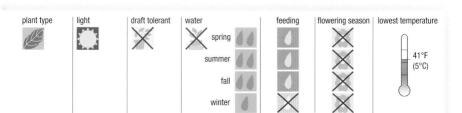

plant type	light	draft tolerant	water		feeding	flowering season	lowest temperature
			spring				
			summer				41°F (5°C)
			fall				
			winter				

Leptospermum scoparium

Broom Tea Tree/Manuka/Tea Tree

Family: *Myrtaceae*

Use: Flowering shrub for indoors, a greenhouse or sunroom, or outdoors from spring to fall.

Origin: Australia.

Plant description: Flowering shrub with small, silky leaves dotted with fragrant oil glands, and a mass of small, waxy flowers, colored white, pink, or red.

Light and position: Prefers full sunlight; tolerates filtered sun.

Temperature range: Warm to cool, tolerating temperatures down to 32°F (0°C).

Water: The plant tolerates standing in water, but not drying out. Keep the soil constantly moist with soft water.

Feeding: Feed with an acid fertilizer every two weeks from spring to fall. Do not feed during the remainder of the year.

Special care: The plant prefers a dormant period during winter, when it should be kept in a light, cool position, at about 41–50°F (5–10°C). The formation of flowers is promoted by short days (less than eight hours of daylight) and low temperatures. Repot in acid soil every year in spring.

Pests and diseases: Fungus disease.

Other species/cultivars: There is a wide variety of cultivars, with flower colors ranging from white to red.

Propagation: Stem cuttings from semi-ripe shoots can be taken in fall. The cuttings should be placed in a heated propagator or on a propagation blanket, with a bottom heat of 54–68°F (12–20°C).

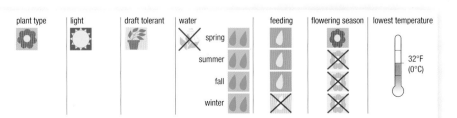

plant type	light	draft tolerant	water		feeding	flowering season	lowest temperature
			spring				
			summer				32°F (0°C)
			fall				
			winter				

Lithops spp.
Living Stones/Stone Plants/Pebble Plants
Family: *Aizoaceae*

Use: Succulent for indoors, a greenhouse, or a sunroom.

Origin: South Africa.

Plant description: Slow-growing succulent with united pairs of swollen leaves that resemble stones. The leaves are often gray or brown, with intense patterning. Brightly colored, daisy-like flowers appear in summer.

Light and position: Prefers full sun.

Temperature range: Warm, cooler in winter. Tolerates temperatures down to 36°F (2°C).

Water: Water regularly from spring to fall, letting the soil dry out thoroughly before watering again. Do not water during winter when the plant is dormant. Start to water sparingly again in spring, when the new leaves appear. This plant will rot and die if overwatered.

Feeding: Feed with a weak fertilizer once a month from spring to fall. Do not feed during the remainder of the year.

Special care: This succulent will die if it is watered too much or placed in poor light conditions. It prefers a dormant period during winter, when it should be kept at 46–50°F (8–10°C). Repot every third year in early spring, using a fertilizer-free potting mixture. Place small stones around the plant, on top of the soil, to ensure good drainage.

Pests and diseases: Fungus disease will kill this plant if it is overwatered.

Other species/cultivars: There are many species, with different shapes and colors of leaves and flowers.

Propagation: Sow seeds in fall or spring, or take stem cuttings in spring.

plant type

light

draft tolerant

water

spring   summer   fall   winter

feeding

flowering season

lowest temperature

36°F
(2°C)

Ludisia discolor
Jewel Orchid

Family: *Orchidaceae*

plant type

light

draft tolerant

water

spring summer fall winter

feeding

flowering season

lowest temperature

55°F
(13°C)

Use: Flowering orchid for indoors, a greenhouse, or a sunroom.
Origin: South China, Vietnam, and Malay Peninsula.
Plant description: Small, terrestrial orchid with creeping rhizomes and velvety, oval leaves, colored dark green with red veining. The small flowers are white and fragrant.
Light and position: Filtered sunlight to shade. Keep the plant away from direct sunlight.
Temperature range: Warm to cool, tolerating temperatures down to 55°F (13°C).

Water: Keep the soil constantly moist with soft water, as this plant does not tolerate drying out. Mist frequently with a hand-spray to maintain high humidity.
Feeding: Feed with a special orchid fertilizer during the flowering period. Do not feed during the remainder of the year.
Special care: Repot every second or third year in spring, using orchid compost.
Pests and diseases: Scale insects, spider mites, and fungus disease.
Other species/cultivars: None.
Propagation: Stem-tip cuttings can be taken in spring. Leave them in a cool, dry place for 48 hours before potting in orchid compost. The cuttings should be placed in a heated propagator, set to high humidity and a bottom heat of 68°F (20°C).

Mandevilla (hybrids)

Family: *Apocynaceae*

Use: Flowering climber for indoors, a greenhouse or sunroom, or outdoors. Suitable for a small trellis.

Plant description: Twining climber with shiny, dark green leaves and trumpet-shaped flowers, which may be whitish, pink, or dark pink and display a deep rose eye. The plant has a milky sap.

Light and position: Prefers full sunlight; tolerates filtered sun.

Temperature range: Warm to cool, tolerating temperatures down to 41°F (5°C).

Water: Water regularly from spring to fall, allowing the soil to dry out slightly before watering again. The soil should be drier if the plant is kept cool during winter.

Feeding: Feed with a low-nitrogen fertilizer every two weeks from spring to fall. Do not feed during the remainder of the year.

Special care: The sap may cause irritation to the skin. This climber needs support so is ideal for a small trellis. It prefers a dormant period during winter, when it should be kept in a light, cool position at about 50–59°F (10–15°C). Repot every year in early spring; long shoots can be cut back at the same time.

Pests and diseases: Aphids and spider mites.

Other species/cultivars: *M. amoena* 'Alice duPont' bears showy flowers in summer. *M. boliviensis* has smaller flowers, colored pure white with an orange-yellow throat. *M. sanderi* is smaller in plant and leaf size, and bears flowers in shades of pink with a yellow throat.

Propagation: Take stem cuttings from softwood or greenwood in early spring. The cuttings should be placed in a heated propagator or on a propagation blanket, with a bottom heat of 68–77°F (20–25°C).

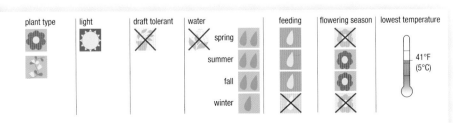

plant type	light	draft tolerant	water		feeding	flowering season	lowest temperature
				spring			41°F (5°C)
				summer			
				fall			
				winter			

plant type

light

draft tolerant

water

spring summer fall winter

feeding

flowering season

lowest temperature

59°F
(15°C)

Maranta leuconeura
Prayer Plant/Rabbit Tracks
Family: *Marantaceae*

Use: Ornamental foliage plant for indoors, or a greenhouse or sunroom in summer. Ideal for use as groundcover.

Origin: Brazil.

Plant description: Compact, perennial herb with oval, gray-green leaves that curl up in the evening. The leaves display a row of dark brown blotches on each side of the midrib.

Light and position: Prefers a shady to filtered-sun position. Keep away from direct sunlight.

Temperature range: Warm, tolerating temperatures down to 59°F (15°C).

Water: Keep the soil constantly moist. This plant tolerates only a slight drying out. Mist frequently with a hand-spray to maintain high humidity.

Feeding: Feed with a low-nitrogen fertilizer once a month from spring to fall. Do not feed during the remainder of the year.

Special care: This plant prefers high humidity. Repot every second year in early spring.

Pests and diseases: Spider mites.

Other species/cultivars: The cultivar 'Fascinator' has pink veins forming a fishbone pattern.

Propagation: Divide the plant or take basal stem cuttings in spring.

plant type

light

draft tolerant

water

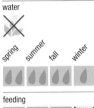

feeding

flowering season

lowest temperature

54°F
(12°C)

Miltonia

Miltonia/Pansy Orchid (hybrids)

Family: *Orchidaceae*

Use: Flowering orchid for indoors, a greenhouse, or a sunroom.

Origin: Brazil.

Plant description: Epiphytic orchid with long leaves and pseudobulbs (thickened, bulb-like stems). The erect stalks bear large, purple and white flowers that resemble the flowers of garden pansies.

Light and position: Filtered sunlight. Keep the plant away from full sun.

Temperature range: Warm to cool, tolerating temperatures down to 54°F (12°C).

Water: Water regularly with soft water from spring to fall, and avoid letting the soil dry out. Water more sparingly during winter.

Feeding: Feed once a month with an orchid fertilizer from spring to summer. Do not feed during the remainder of the year.

Special care: Repot the plant in a small container every year in spring, using special orchid compost.

Pests and diseases: Scale insects, spider mites, and fungus disease.

Other species/cultivars: Many species and cultivars are grown, varying in flower shape and color.

Propagation: Remove and repot the leafless back bulb in spring.

plant type

light

draft tolerant

water

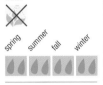

spring summer fall winter

feeding

flowering season

lowest temperature

59°F
(15°C)

Monstera deliciosa

Swiss Cheese Plant/
TaroVine/Windowleaf/Ceriman/
Mexican Breadfruit

Family: *Araceae*

Use: A sculptural, foliage plant for indoors, or a greenhouse or sunroom in summer.

Origin: Mexico.

Plant description: Woody climber with large, glossy, green leaves, leathery in texture, and long aerial roots. The leaves have no indentations when young, but later become pinnate and acquire holes.

Light and position: Tolerates a broad spectrum of light, but should be kept away from full sun.

Temperature range: Prefers a warm position, but tolerates temperatures down to 59°F (15°C).

Water: Water regularly all year round. The plant does not tolerate drying out, which may cause leaf burn.

Feeding: Feed with a low-nitrogen fertilizer every two weeks from spring to fall. Do not feed during the remainder of the year.

Special care: This is a large plant that requires space. It benefits from a monthly shower in the bathroom. The plant can be cut back in spring and should be repotted every second or third year in early spring.

Pests and diseases: Aphids, spider mites, and gray mold.

Other species/cultivars: None.

Propagation: Leaf-bud or stem cuttings two nodes in length can be taken at any time of year. The cuttings should be placed in a heated propagator or on a propagation blanket, set to high humidity and a bottom heat of 68–77°F (20–25°C).

Plant type

plant type

light

draft tolerant

water

spring summer fall winter

feeding

flowering season

lowest temperature

41°F
(5°C)

Myrtus communis

Myrtle

Family: *Myrtaceae*

Use: Aromatic foliage plant for indoors, a greenhouse or sunroom, or outdoors from spring to fall.

Origin: Europe.

Plant description: Evergreen shrub with leathery, shiny dark-green leaves, broadly ovate in shape, which are aromatic when crushed. The plant sometimes bears fragrant, white flowers with a mass of white stamens, and these may be followed by purple berries.

Light and position: Prefers full sunlight; tolerates filtered sun.

Temperature range: Warm to cool, tolerating temperatures down to 41°F (5°C). The plant prefers a cool position during winter.

Water: Water regularly with soft water from spring to fall, more sparingly during the rest of the year. Avoid letting the soil dry out.

Feeding: Feed with a low-nitrogen fertilizer every two weeks from spring to fall. Do not feed during the remainder of the year.

Special care: The plant prefers a dormant period during winter, when it should be kept in a light, cool position at about 41–50°F (5–10°C). Repot every second year in spring; the shrub may be cut back at the same time.

Pests and diseases: Mealy bugs, scale insects, and white fly.

Other species/cultivars: None.

Propagation: Stem cuttings from semi-ripe shoots to hardwood can be taken in fall.

Nematanthus gregarius
Clog Plant/Goldfish Plant
Family: *Gesneriaceae*

Use: Flowering shrub for indoors, a greenhouse, or a sunroom.

Origin: Mexico, Guatemala, Costa Rica, and Panama.

Plant description: Tough, branching or erect shrub with small, glossy, succulent leaves. Solitary, fleshy, pitcher-like flowers, colored orange-yellow, are produced in the plant's leaf-axils.

Light and position: Full sunlight to filtered sun.

Temperature range: Warm to cool, tolerating temperatures down to 41°F (5°C). The plant prefers a cool position during winter.

Water: Water regularly during growing season by standing the pot in water for ten minutes. Allow the soil to dry out slightly before watering again. Water more sparingly during the rest of the year.

Feeding: Feed with a low-nitrogen fertilizer every two weeks from spring to fall. Do not feed during the remainder of the year.

Special care: Old plants will flower permanently for years. The plant prefers a dormant period during winter, when it should be kept in a light, cool position at about 50–59°F (10–15°C). Repot in early spring, and cut back long shoots at the same time.

Pests and diseases: Aphids, spider mites, gray mold, and mealy dew.

Other species/cultivars: None.

Propagation: Stem cuttings can be taken in spring.

plant type	light	draft tolerant	water		feeding	flowering season	lowest temperature
			spring				
			summer				41°F (5°C)
			fall				
			winter				

plant type

light

draft tolerant

water

spring summer fall winter

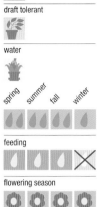

feeding

flowering season

lowest temperature

46°F
(8°C)

Neoregelia carolinae
Blushing Bromeliad

Family: *Bromeliaceae*

Use: Tough, flowering bromeliad for indoors, or a greenhouse or sunroom in summer.

Origin: Brazil.

Plant description: Flowering urn-shaped rosette of shiny leaves with a leathery texture and toothed margins. A mass of flowers grow in the rosette, surrounded by shiny red bracts.

Light and position: Tolerates a broad spectrum of light but should be kept away from full sun.

Temperature range: Warm to cool, tolerating temperatures down to 46°F (8°C).

Water: Water with lukewarm water. The plant tolerates drying out for a few weeks.

Feeding: Feed regularly with a weak fertilizer in the rosette from spring to fall. Do not feed during the remainder of the year.

Special care: Water and fertilize inside the rosette, which should always contain water except when the plant is kept at low temperatures. Repot offsets in spring or summer.

Pests and diseases: Mealy bugs and spider mites.

Other species/cultivars:
'Meyendorffii' has olive-green leaves and lilac flowers. 'Flandria' has olive-green leaves with narrow, yellow margins. 'Tricolor Perfecta' has yellow-green leaves with dark green margins.

Propagation: Divide and repot offsets in spring or summer.

Nepenthes
Pitcher Plant (hybrids)

Family: *Nepenthaceae*

Use: Sculptural, insectivorous plant for indoors, or a greenhouse or sunroom in summer. Some cultivars are suitable for hanging baskets.

Plant description: Herbaceous plant with leathery, lance-shaped leaves and unusual hollow "pitchers" with lids, in which insects are trapped and digested. The brown-and-green pitchers develop from the prolonged midribs of the leaves, which function as clinging tendrils.

Light and position: Filtered sunlight. Keep the plant away from full sun.

Temperature range: Warm, tolerating temperatures down to 59°F (15°C).

Water: Only use soft water and avoid letting the soil dry out. Keep the plant constantly moist by misting with a hand-spray.

Feeding: Feed once a week with a very weak fertilizer from spring to fall. The fertilizer should be sprayed on the leaves with a hand-spray.

Special care: This plant prefers high humidity. It should be repotted every year in early spring, in coarse sphagnum mixed with gravel, and may be cut back at the same time.

Pests and diseases: None.

Other species/cultivars: Many different cultivars and species are available, varying in shape, color, and size of pitcher.

Propagation: Sow seeds in spring, placing them in a heated propagator or on a propagation blanket at 81°F (27°C). Cuttings can be taken from semi-ripe shoots in spring.

plant type	light	draft tolerant	water		feeding	flowering season	lowest temperature
				spring			
				summer			59°F
				fall			(15°C)
				winter			

Nephrolepis exaltata
Boston Fern/
Boston Sword Fern

Family: *Nephrolepidaceae*

Use: A sculptural fern for indoors, or a greenhouse or sunroom in summer. Some cultivars are suitable for hanging baskets.

Origin: Tropical.

Plant description: Tough, compact fern with pinnate, fresh-green leaves, which may be drooping or upright.

Light and position: Filtered sunlight. Keep the plant away from full sun during summer.

Temperature range: Prefers a warm position, but tolerates temperatures down to 50°F (10°C).

Water: Water regularly in growing season, allowing the soil to dry out slightly before watering again. Water more sparingly during the rest of the year. Mist the plant frequently with a hand-spray to maintain high humidity.

Feeding: Feed with a low-nitrogen fertilizer every two weeks from spring to fall. Do not feed during the remainder of the year.

Special care: Prefers high humidity. Old leaves may be cut off at any time of year, and the plant should be repotted every second year in spring.

Pests and diseases: Aphids, mealy bugs, scale insects, and gray mold.

Other species/cultivars:
There is a range of cultivars, varying in leaf shape, size, and color. 'Bostoniensis' has drooping, light green leaves. 'Teddy Junior' has dark green leaves with wavy leaflets.

Propagation: The plantlets that develop along the rhizomes may be separated from the parent plant in early spring. Spores may be sown when ripe.

plant type	light	draft tolerant	water		feeding	flowering season	lowest temperature
			spring				50°F (10°C)
			summer				
			fall				
			winter				

Nertera granadensis

Bead Plant/Makole/Coral Moss/
English Babytears

Family: *Rubiaceae*

Use: Foliage herb with berries for indoors, a greenhouse or sunroom, or outdoors in summer. Ideal for groundcover.

Origin: Central America, South America, Australia, and New Zealand.

Plant description: Creeping perennial with tiny, green leaves, forming dense mats of foliage. It bears small, green flowers followed by attractive, round, translucent orange or yellow berries.

Light and position: Filtered sunlight. Keep the plant away from full sun.

Temperature range: Warm to cool, tolerating temperatures down to 41°F (5°C). Prefers a cool position during winter.

Water: Water from underneath, standing the pot in water for ten minutes. Allow the soil to dry out before watering again. The soil should be drier if the plant is kept cool in winter.

Feeding: Feed with a low-nitrogen fertilizer once a month from spring to summer. Do not feed during the remainder of the year.

Special care: Discard the plant when the berries begin to die off. Alternatively, place it in a cooler position during winter, at a temperature of 41–50°F (5–10°C), to promote flower and fruit formation next year. Repot in early spring.

Pests and deseases: Aphids, mealy bugs, and gray mold.

Other species/cultivars: Various cultivars offer different berry colors, in shades of orange or yellow.

Propagation: By plant division in late spring.

plant type

light

draft tolerant

water

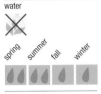

spring summer fall winter

feeding

flowering season

lowest temperature

32°F
(0°C)

Olea europaea
Olive/Edible Olive

Family: *Oleaceae*

Use: Small foliage tree for indoors, a greenhouse or sunroom, or outdoors in summer. The fruit has a culinary use.

Origin: Cultivated since ancient times.

Plant description: Small, evergreen tree with narrow, lance-shaped leaves, leathery in texture and colored gray-green. The insignificant flowers are yellow-white and are followed by olives that are first green and later shiny black. Old pot plants will produce edible olives but require a lot of sunlight and high temperatures to do so.

Light and position: Prefers full sunlight; tolerates filtered sun.

Temperature range: Warm; cooler during winter. Tolerates temperatures down to 32°F (0°C).

Water: Water regularly spring to summer, allowing the soil to dry out slightly before watering again. Keep the soil almost dry in winter.

Feeding: Feed with a low-nitrogen fertilizer once a month from spring to fall. Do not feed during the remainder of the year.

Special care: The tree needs a dormant period during winter, when it should be kept in a light, cool position, at about 41–50°F (5–10°C). It can be cut back in early spring and should be repotted every third year, in early spring.

Pests and diseases: Aphids and scale insects.

Other species/cultivars: None.

Propagation: Stem cuttings from semi-ripe shoots can be taken in summer. The cuttings should be placed in a heated propagator or on a propagation blanket, with a bottom heat of 68–77°F (20–25°C).

Dancing Ladies/Oncidium (hybrids)

Family: *Orchidaceae*

Use: Flowering orchid for indoors, a greenhouse, or a sunroom.

Plant description: Epiphytic orchid with one or two leafed pseudobulbs (thickened, bulb-like stems) and a mass of small orchid flowers arranged in branching sprays. The flowers are vivid yellow, usually marked with a red-brown blotch at the base of each segment.

Light and position: Filtered sunlight; keep the plant away from full sun.

Temperature range: Warm when flowering, cooler during the rest of the year. Tolerates temperatures down to 50°F (10°C).

Water: Water regularly with soft water during flowering, allowing the soil to dry out slightly before watering again. Letting water stand around bulbs and roots may cause fungus disease. Mist frequently with a hand-spray to maintain high humidity.

Feeding: Feed once a month with an orchid fertilizer from spring to fall. Do not feed during the rest of the year.

Special care: After flowering, the orchid needs a rest period before it can flower again. Keep the plant in a light, cool place for a few weeks, at about 50–59°F (10–15°C), and water very sparingly until new flowering buds can be seen. Repot in early spring only if the pseudobulbs need more space, using special orchid compost.

Pests and diseases: Scale insects, spider mites, and fungus disease.

Other species/cultivars: There are many cultivars, ranging in flower color from yellow to purple. *O. ornithorynchum* bears small, strongly scented, rose to pink flowers.

Propagation: In spring, remove and pot the back bulb.

plant type	light	draft tolerant	water		feeding	flowering season	lowest temperature
			spring				
			summer				50°F
			fall				(10°C)
			winter				

Ornithogalum thyrsoides
Chincherinchee/Wonder Flower

Family: *Hyacinthaceae*

Use: Flowering bulb for indoors, a greenhouse or sunroom, or outdoors in summer.

Origin: South Africa.

Plant description: Winter-flowering bulb with fleshy, lance-shaped leaves and erect racemes clustering a mass of long-lasting, white flowers with dark hearts.

Light and position: Prefers full sunlight; tolerates filtered sun.

Temperature range: Warm, cooler during winter. Tolerates temperatures down to 32°F (0°C).

Water: This plant will rot and die if overwatered. Water regularly, allowing the soil to dry out before watering again.

Feeding: None.

Special care: Discard the plant after flowering, or place or plant it in the garden. The bulb is easy to grow but difficult to make flower again.

Pests and diseases: Fungus disease.

Other species/cultivars: *O. longibracteatum* grows a showy, large, light green bulb above the soil. *O. dubium* bears bright orange flowers.

Propagation: Offsets are divided in fall.

plant type

light

draft tolerant

water

spring summer fall winter

feeding

flowering season

lowest temperature

32°F
(0°C)

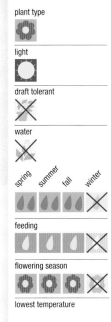

plant type

light

draft tolerant

water

spring summer fall winter

feeding

flowering season

lowest temperature

41°F
(5°C)

Oxalis triangularis

Shamrock/Sorrel

Family: *Oxalidaceae*

Use: Foliage herb for indoors, a greenhouse or sunroom, or outdoors in summer.

Origin: Brazil.

Plant description: Small perennial with long-stalked leaves, each with three forked, green or purple segments. The flowers are white or rose.

Light and position: Filtered sunlight; keep the plant away from full sun.

Temperature range: Warm, cooler during winter. Tolerates temperatures down to 41°F (5°C).

Water: Water regularly, allowing the soil to dry out slightly before watering again. The plant tolerates drying out and should be kept dry when dormant.

Feeding: Feed with a low-nitrogen fertilizer once a month from spring to fall. Do not feed during the remainder of the year.

Special care: This plant prefers a dormant period during winter. Stop watering in fall, and let the plant wither. Keep the rhizomes in their pot, in a dry, cool position at about 41–50°F (5–10°C). In spring, repot the rhizomes, place them in a warmer position and start watering again.

Pests and diseases: Aphids, white fly, and gray mold.

Other species/cultivars: *O. adenophylla* bears lilac-pink flowers and leaves with multiple leaflets. *O. articulata* has rose flower clusters and light green leaves with three segments. *O. deppei* has rose-red flowers and large leaves with four segments and brown-purple marking.

Propagation: Division of rhizomes can take place in early spring.

Pachira aquatica
Provision Tree/
Water Chestnut/Guiana Chestnut

Family: *Bombacaceae*

Use: Sculptural tree for indoors, or a greenhouse or sunroom in summer. Rare.

Origin: South Mexico, Central America, and tropical South America.

Plant description: Tough tree with a woody trunk, swollen at the base, and large, stalked leaves with many oval leaflets. Small sugar crystals form on the underside of the leaves; these are harmless to the plant.

Light and position: Prefers full sunlight; tolerates filtered sun.

Temperature range: Warm, tolerating temperatures down to 59°F (15°C).

Water: Water regularly, allowing the soil to dry out slightly before watering again. The plant tolerates drying out.

Feeding: Feed with a low-nitrogen fertilizer every two weeks from spring to fall. Do not feed during the remainder of the year.

Special care: Repot every year in early spring. The tree can be cut back and shaped at the same time.

Pests and diseases: Aphids and scale insects.

Other species/cultivars: None.

Propagation: Seeds can be sown in spring.

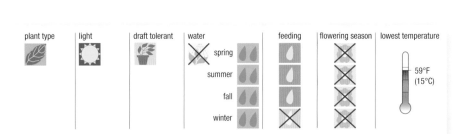

plant type	light	draft tolerant	water		feeding	flowering season	lowest temperature
			spring	💧💧	💧	✕	59°F (15°C)
			summer	💧💧	💧	✕	
			fall	💧💧	💧	✕	
			winter	💧💧	✕	✕	

Paphiopedilum
Slipper Orchid/Venus' Slipper (hybrids)
Family: *Orchidaceae*

Use: Flowering orchid for indoors, a greenhouse, or a sunroom.

Plant description: Terrestrial orchid with basal leaves and a long-lasting, waxy flower, which may be different shades of shiny brown, green, yellow, orange, or purple.

Light and position: Filtered sunlight; keep the plant away from full sun.

Temperature range: Warm, tolerating temperatures down to 59°F (15°C).

Water: Water regularly with soft water from spring to fall, and avoid letting the soil dry out. Water more sparingly during winter.

Feeding: Feed once a month with orchid fertilizer from spring to fall. Do not feed during the remainder of the year.

Special care: This orchid does not need a rest period. Repot every year in spring in a small container, using orchid compost.

Pests and diseases: Scale insects, spider mites, and fungus disease.

Other species/cultivars: Many species and cultivars are grown, offering a variety of flower shapes and colors.

Propagation: The clumps can be divided by separating small plants when repotting.

plant type

light

draft tolerant

water

spring	summer	fall	winter

feeding

flowering season

lowest temperature

59°F
(15°C)

Plant type

light

draft tolerant

water

spring summer fall winter

feeding

flowering season

lowest temperature

14°F
(-10°C)

Passiflora caerulea

Blue Passion Flower/
Passion Flower

Family: *Passifloraceae*

Use: Flowering climber for indoors, a greenhouse or sunroom, or outdoors. Ideal for a trellis or hoop.

Origin: South Brazil, Paraguay, and Argentina.

Plant description: Vigorous climber growing stems that may be up to 33 ft (10 m) long. It bears distinctive, solitary flowers, with bright white sepals and petals and blue, white, and purple corona filaments arranged four rows deep. The leaves are palmate, with five or seven lobes.

Light and position: Prefers full sunlight; tolerates filtered sun.

Temperature range: Prefers a cool, sunny position, and tolerates a few degrees of frost.

Water: Water regularly from spring to fall, and avoid letting the soil dry out. Water more sparingly during the winter dormant period, as the plant will die if overwatered.

Feeding: Feed every two weeks with a low-nitrogen fertilizer from spring to fall. Do not feed during the remainder of the year.

Special care: This climber needs support, so is suitable for a trellis or training to a hoop. Night temperatures below 64°F (18°C) are required to promote the formation of flowers. Cut back any long shoots in fall, and allow the plant a dormant period during winter, when it should be kept in a light, cool position at about 41–50°F (5–10°C).

Pests and diseases: Aphids and spider mites.

Other species/cultivars: Many species and cultivars are grown. *P. citrina* bears medium-sized, yellow flowers. *P. vitifolia* has vine-like leaves and crimson flowers.

Propagation: Stem cuttings from semi-ripe shoots or softwood can be taken from spring to summer.

Pelargonium x *domesticum*
Regal Pelargonium/Regal Geranium

Family: *Geraniaceae*

Use: Flowering shrub for indoors, a greenhouse or sunroom, or outdoors from spring to fall.

Plant description: Compact shrub with erect, hairy stems and large, hairy leaves, which may be toothed or lobed. The large flowers are found in a broad range of colors, from white to salmon, pink, red, or purple.

Light and position: Prefers filtered sunlight; tolerates full sun.

Temperature range: Warm to cool, preferring a cool position. Tolerates temperatures down to 32°F (0°C).

Water: Water regularly in the growing season, allowing the soil to dry out before watering again. Water more sparingly during the rest of the year, especially when the plant is kept cool.

Feeding: Feed with a low-nitrogen fertilizer every two weeks from spring to fall. Do not feed during the remainder of the year.

Special care: Cut back the plant in fall to promote more compact growth. As flower formation is induced by low temperatures, the plant must be placed in a cool position, at 41–50°F (5–10°C), for at least eight weeks during winter. In early spring, repot and place in a warmer position.

Pests and diseases: Aphids, spider mites, white fly, gray mold, and mildew.

Other species/cultivars: The 'Angel' cultivars have smaller flowers and often scented leaves.

Propagation: Cuttings from softwood can be taken from spring to fall; cuttings of semi-ripe shoots, from summer to fall.

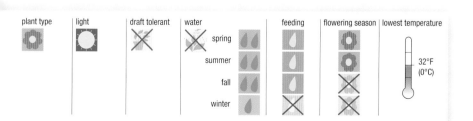

plant type	light	draft tolerant	water		feeding	flowering season	lowest temperature
			spring				
			summer				32°F (0°C)
			fall				
			winter				

Pelargonium x hortorum
Bedding Geranium/Zonal Pelargonium
Family: *Geraniaceae*

Use: Flowering shrub for indoors, a greenhouse or sunroom, or outdoors from spring to fall.

Plant description: Branching shrub with smooth or hairy, almost circular leaves, which are sometimes scented and usually marked with a purple ring. The flowers are clustered in umbels and come in a broad range of colors, from white to salmon, pink, red, or purple.

Light and position: Prefers full sunlight; tolerates filtered sun.

Temperature range: Warm to cool, preferring a cool position. Tolerates temperatures down to 32°F (0°C).

Water: Water regularly in growing season, allowing the soil to dry out before watering again. Water more sparingly during the rest of the year, especially when the plant is kept cool.

Feeding: Feed with a low-nitrogen fertilizer every two weeks from spring to fall. Do not feed during the remainder of the year.

Special care: Cut back the plant in fall to promote a more compact growth. It prefers a cool position during winter, at 41–50°F (5–10°C). Repot in early spring and place in a warmer position.

Pests and diseases: Aphids, spider mites, white fly, gray mold, and mildew.

Other species/cultivars: Numerous cultivars are found, varying in flower color.

Propagation: Cuttings from softwood can be taken from spring to fall; cuttings of semi-ripe shoots, from summer to fall.

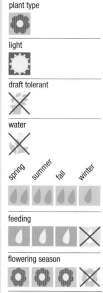

plant type

light

draft tolerant

water

spring summer fall winter

feeding

flowering season

lowest temperature

32°F
(0°C)

Pellaea rotundifolia
Button Fern
Family: *Adiantaceae*

Use: Ornamental fern for indoors, or a greenhouse or sunroom in summer. Ideal for use as groundcover.

Origin: New Zealand and Norfolk Islands.

Plant description: Compact fern with a creeping rootstock and hairy stems. The pendant leaves are pinnate, with waxy, dark green leaflets, round to ovate in shape.

Light and position: Filtered sunlight to shade. Keep the plant away from direct sunlight.

Temperature range: Warm to cool, preferring a cool position during winter. Tolerates temperatures down to 50°F (10°C).

Water: The soil should be kept constantly moist, especially during growing season, but the plant will not tolerate overwatering. Mist the leaves frequently with a hand-spray to maintain high humidity.

Feeding: Feed with a low-nitrogen fertilizer once a month from spring to fall. Do not feed during the remainder of the year.

Special care: This plant enjoys high humidity. It also prefers a dormant period during winter, when it should be kept in a dry, cool position at about 59°F (15°C). Repot every second year in early spring.

Pests and diseases: Aphids, scale insects, spider mites, and gray mold.

Other species/cultivars: *P. falcata* has linear, pinnate leaves with sickle-shaped leaflets.

Propagation: By spores.

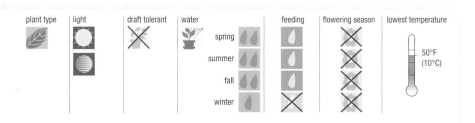

plant type	light	draft tolerant	water		feeding	flowering season	lowest temperature
				spring			
				summer			50°F (10°C)
				fall			
				winter			

Peperomia argyreia
Watermelon Pepper/Watermelon Begonia

Family: *Piperaceae*

Use: Ornamental foliage for indoors, or a greenhouse or sunroom in summer.

Origin: Tropical South America.

Plant description: Compact, herbaceous perennial cultivated for its ornamental leaves. It has a short, erect stem and fleshy, shiny, silver-green leaves, similar in coloring to a watermelon. The leaves are marked with dark green along their veins.

Light and position: Tolerates a shady to filtered sun position. Keep away from direct sunlight.

Temperature range: Warm to cool, tolerating temperatures down to 59°F (15°C).

Water: Water regularly, allowing the soil to dry out slightly before watering again. This plant will rot and die if overwatered. Mist the leaves frequently with a hand-spray to maintain high humidity.

Feeding: Feed with a low-nitrogen fertilizer once a month from spring to fall. Do not feed during the remainder of the year.

Special care: This plant is easy to grow. It prefers high humidity and should be repotted every year in early spring. At the same time, it can be cut back to promote a more compact growth.

Pests and diseases: Aphids, scale insects, spider mites, white fly, and gray mold.

Other species/cultivars: Many other species and cultivars are grown. *P. arifolia* has large, shiny grass-green leaves with pointed tips.

Propagation: Stem-tip or leaf cuttings can be taken from softwood at any time of year. To root the cuttings, place them in a heated propagator or on a propagation blanket at 70°F (21°C).

plant type

light

draft tolerant

water

spring summer fall winter

feeding

flowering season

lowest temperature

59°F
(15°C)

Peperomia caperata
Emerald Ripple/Emerald-Ripple Pepper/
Green-Ripple Pepper/ Little-Fantasy Pepper

Family: *Piperaceae*

Use: Ornamental foliage for indoors, or a greenhouse or sunroom in summer.
Origin: Brazil.
Plant description: Tough, compact, herbaceous perennial. It is almost stemless and forms dense clusters of fleshy, quilted leaves, round to heart-shaped, with fleshy, reddish leaf-stalks. Small, creamy-white flower spikes are sometimes produced.
Light and position: Tolerates a shady to filtered sun position. Keep away from direct sunlight.
Temperature range: Warm to cool, tolerating temperatures down to 59°F (15°C).
Water: Water regularly, allowing the soil to dry out slightly before watering again. The plant will rot and die if overwatered. Mist the leaves frequently with a hand-spray to maintain high humidity.

Feeding: Feed with a low-nitrogen fertilizer once a month from spring to fall. Do not feed during the remainder of the year. Excessive feeding will lessen the intensity of the leaf coloring.
Special care: This plant is easy to grow. It prefers high humidity and should be repotted every year in early spring. At the same time, it can be cut back to promote a more compact growth.
Pests and diseases: Aphids, scale insects, spider mites, white fly, and gray mold.
Other species/cultivars: The cultivars vary in leaf size and color, ranging from dark green, like 'Liliana,' to dark red, creamy, pinkish, or white-margined.
Propagation: Stem-tip or leaf cuttings can be taken from softwood at any time of year. To root the cuttings, place them in a heated propagator or on a propagation blanket at 70°F (21°C).

plant type

light

draft tolerant

water

spring summer fall winter

feeding

flowering season

lowest temperature

59°F
(15°C)

Pericallis
Cineraria/Florist's Cineraria (x hybrids)
Family: *Asteraceae*

Use: Flowering ornamental for indoors, a greenhouse, or a sunroom.

Plant description: Compact herb with large, grass-green leaves, tinged with blue or purple on the underside, and a dense cluster of large, daisy-like flowers. The flowers range in color from white to orange, pink, purple, or blue, often with a contrasting circle surrounding the central disc.

Light and position: Full sunlight to filtered sun.

Temperature range: Warm to cool, tolerating temperatures down to 50°F (10°C). The flowers will last longer if the plant is kept in a cool position, at 50–59°F (10–15°C).

Water: Keep the soil constantly moist, as the plant will collapse if its roots dry out. Water from underneath, standing the pot in water for ten minutes.

Feeding: None.

Special care: Discard the plant after flowering. Repotting is unnecessary as the plant will flower only once.

Pests and diseases: Aphids, mildew, and gray mold.

Other species/cultivars: Cultivars offer a variety of flower colors.

Propagation: Seeds are sown in spring.

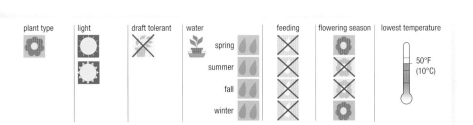

plant type	light	draft tolerant	water		feeding	flowering season	lowest temperature
			spring				50°F (10°C)
			summer				
			fall				
			winter				

Phalaenopsis
Moth Orchid (hybrids)

Family: *Orchidaceae*

Use: Flowering orchid for indoors, a greenhouse, or a sunroom.

Plant description: Epiphytic orchid with leathery basal leaves and a pendant, often elongated inflorescence with a mass of flowers in a broad range of colors, from white to yellow, greenish, pink, or purple.

Light and position: Filtered sunlight. Keep the plant away from full sun.

Temperature range: Prefers a warm position but tolerates temperatures down to 59°F (15°C).

Water: Water regularly, allowing the soil to dry out slightly before watering again. This plant prefers soft water. Avoid letting water stand around the bulbs and roots, which may cause fungus disease. Mist the leaves frequently with a hand-spray.

Feeding: Feed with an orchid fertilizer once a month from spring to fall. Do not feed during the remainder of the year.

Special care: This orchid will flower for a long time. When the flowers have withered, cut off the inflorescence above the second flower to allow a new inflorescence to grow. Repot the orchid, using orchid compost, when the pot is full of roots and flowering is over.

Pests and diseases: Scale insects, spider mites, and fungus disease.

Other species/cultivars: There are many cultivars, varying in size and flower color. 'Petit Avenir' has numerous small, purple and white flowers.

Propagation: Remove and repot rooted plantlets at any time of year.

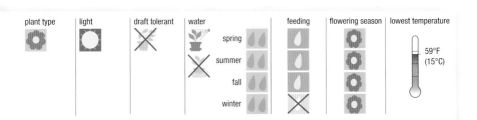

plant type	light	draft tolerant	water		feeding	flowering season	lowest temperature
			spring				
			summer				59°F (15°C)
			fall				
			winter				

plant type

light

draft tolerant

water

spring summer fall winter

feeding

flowering season

lowest temperature

59°F
(15°C)

Philodendron erubescens

Blushing Philodendron/
Red-leaf Philodendron

Family: *Araceae*

Use: Ornamental foliage for indoors, or a greenhouse or sunroom in summer. Ideal for training around a pole.

Origin: Colombia.

Plant description: Compact, erect climber with large, arrow-shaped leaves, colored glossy green or red-green.

Light and position: Tolerates a shady to filtered sun position. Keep away from direct sunlight.

Temperature range: Warm to cool, tolerating temperatures down to 59°F (15°C).

Water: Keep the soil constantly moist. The plant tolerates only a slight drying out. Mist frequently with a hand-spray to maintain high humidity.

Feeding: Feed with a low-nitrogen fertilizer every two weeks from spring to fall. Do not feed during the remainder of the year.

Special care: This plant needs support, such as a pole. It prefers high humidity and can be cut back at any time of year to promote a more compact growth. Repot every third year in early spring.

Pests and diseases: Aphids, spider mites, and gray mold.

Other species/cultivars: 'Imperial Red' has large, dark green leaves. 'Red Emerald' has smaller, dark green leaves.

Propagation: Stem or stem-tip cuttings can be taken from softwood or semi-ripe shoots all year round. The cuttings should be placed in a heated propagator or on a propagation blanket, with a bottom heat of 70–77°F (21–25°C).

Philodendron
scandens

Heartleaf Philodendron

Family: *Araceae*

Use: Tough foliage climber for indoors, or a greenhouse or sunroom in summer. Ideal for a hanging basket or for trailing.

Origin: East Mexico and Panama.

Plant description: Climbing, stem-rooting vine with dark green, heart-shaped leaves.

Light and position: Tolerates a shady to filtered-sun position. Keep away from direct sunlight.

Temperature range: Warm to cool, tolerating temperatures down to 59°F (15°C).

Water: Keep the soil constantly moist. This plant tolerates only a slight drying out. Mist the leaves frequently with a hand-spray to maintain high humidity.

Feeding: Feed with a low-nitrogen fertilizer every two weeks from spring to fall. Do not feed during the remainder of the year.

Special care: This plant needs support, such as a hanging basket. It prefers high humidity. Long shoots can be cut back at any time of year to make the growth more compact. Repot every third year in early spring.

Pests and diseases: Aphids, spider mites, and gray mold.

Other species/cultivars: None.

Propagation: Stem or stem-tip cuttings can be taken from softwood or semi-ripe shoots all year round. The cuttings should be placed in a heated propagator or on a propagation blanket, with a bottom heat of 70–77°F (21–25°C).

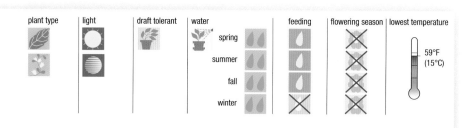

plant type	light	draft tolerant	water		feeding	flowering season	lowest temperature
				spring			59°F (15°C)
				summer			
				fall			
				winter			

Platycerium bifurcatum

Staghorn Fern/
Elkhorn Fern

Family: *Polypodiaceae*

Use: A sculptural fern for indoors, or a greenhouse or sunroom in summer.

Origin: New Guinea and Australia.

Plant description: Tough, epiphytic fern with two kinds of leaves. The upper, fertile leaves are gray-green and resemble stag horns, with absorbent, star-shaped hairs on the underside. The lower leaves are shield-shaped and are green when young and brown and parchment-like later.

Light and position: Prefers a shady position. Keep away from direct sunlight.

Temperature range: Warm to cool, preferring a cool position in winter. Tolerates temperatures down to 45°F (7°C).

Water: Water regularly in growing season, allowing the soil to dry out before watering again. Water more sparingly during the rest of the year. This plant will rot and die if overwatered.

Feeding: Feed with a low-nitrogen fertilizer once a month from spring to fall. Do not feed during the remainder of the year.

Special care: Humus accumulates naturally below the lower leaves and from here the fern will absorb water and fertilizer. Older plants can be grown on a piece of bark: wrap the root ball in sphagnum moss and tie it to the bark. This plant prefers a cool position during winter, at about 50–59°F (10–15°C). Repot every second year in early spring.

Pests and diseases: Scale insects and fungus disease.

Other species/cultivars: *P. superbum* is a bigger plant with large, erect lower leaves that are deeply lobed at the top margins.

Propagation: From spores, or repot plantlets when they form distinct nests. Plants must be more than three years old to produce spores.

plant type

light

draft tolerant

water

spring summer fall winter

feeding

flowering season

lowest temperature

45°F (7°C)

Polyscias filicifolia

Fernleaf Aralia

Family: *Araliaceae*

Use: Sculptural foliage shrub for indoors, or a greenhouse or sunroom in summer.

Origin: Pacific Islands.

Plant description: Trunk-forming shrub with fern-like, leathery leaves separated into narrow lobes.

Light and position: Tolerates a broad spectrum of light including full sun.

Temperature range: Prefers a warm position, but tolerates temperatures down to 54°F (12°C).

Water: Water regularly in growing season, allowing the soil to dry out before watering again. Water more sparingly during the rest of the year. This plant will rot and die if overwatered.

Feeding: Feed with a low-nitrogen fertilizer once a month from spring to fall. Do not feed during the remainder of the year.

Special care: The shrub can be cut back in early spring. Repot every second or third year in early spring.

Pests and diseases: Aphids, mealy bugs, scale insects, white fly, and gray mold.

Other species/cultivars: See *P. scutellaria* on p.209. *P. guilfoylei* has gray-green, bi-pinnate leaves.

Propagation: Stem cuttings can be taken in spring. The cuttings should be placed in a heated propagator or on a propagation blanket, with a bottom heat of 68–77°F (20–25°C).

plant type

light

draft tolerant

water

spring summer fall winter

feeding

flowering season

lowest temperature

54°F
(12°C)

Polyscias scutellaria

Dinner Plate Aralia/

Balfour Aralia

Family: *Araliaceae*

Use: Sculptural foliage shrub for indoors, or a greenhouse or sunroom in summer.

Origin: New Caledonia.

Plant description: Trunk-forming, bushy shrub with heart-shaped, leathery leaves that may be purple-green or dark green with white borders.

Light and position: Tolerates a broad spectrum of light including full sun.

Temperature range: Prefers a warm position, but tolerates temperatures down to 54°F (12°C).

Water: Water regularly in growing season, allowing the soil to dry out before watering again. Water more sparingly during the rest of the year. This plant will rot and die if overwatered.

Feeding: Feed with a low-nitrogen fertilizer once a month from spring to fall. Do not feed during the remainder of the year.

Special care: The plant, including its woody trunk, can be cut back in early spring. Repot every second or third year in early spring.

Pests and diseases: Aphids, mealy bugs, scale insects, white fly, and gray mold.

Other species/cultivars: See *P. filicifolia* on p.208. *P. guilfoylei* has gray-green, bi-pinnate leaves.

Propagation: Stem cuttings can be taken in spring. The cuttings should be placed in a heated propagator or on a propagation blanket, with a bottom heat of 68–77°F (20–25°C).

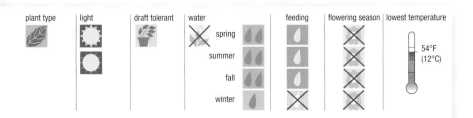

plant type	light	draft tolerant	water		feeding	flowering season	lowest temperature
			spring			✕	
			summer			✕	54°F (12°C)
			fall			✕	
			winter		✕	✕	

plant type

light

draft tolerant

water

spring summer fall winter

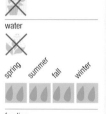

feeding

flowering season

lowest temperature

41°F
(5°C)

Primula obconica

German Primrose/Poison Primrose

Family: *Primulaceae*

Use: Flowering ornamental for indoors, a greenhouse or sunroom, or outdoors.

Origin: China.

Plant description: Herbaceous perennial with large, hairy, broadly heart-shaped leaves and large primrose flowers in pastel shades of white, pink, salmon, rose, orange, or purple, clustered in showy umbels.

Light and position: Filtered sunlight. Keep the plant away from full sun.

Temperature range: Warm to cool, tolerating temperatures down to 41°F (5°C). The flowers will last longer if the plant is kept in a cool position.

Water: Water regularly, allowing the soil to dry out slightly before watering again.

Feeding: Feed with a low-nitrogen fertilizer once a month during flowering season.

Special care: Some people are allergic to the substance primine that is excreted by the hairy glands of this plant. In case of allergic reaction, discard the plant and seek medical advice. In the fall, cut back the flowering stems and place the plant in a cool position, at 41–50°F (5–10°C). Repot in early spring, and the plant will flower again.

Pests and diseases: Aphids, spider mites, and gray mold.

Other species/cultivars: *P. vulgaris* has wrinkled, oblong, basal leaves and many solitary primrose flowers that are found in a broad range of colors. *P. malacoides* has a rosette of long-stalked leaves with white hairs underneath, and pink, rose, and white flowers arranged in successive umbels.

Propagation: Seeds can be sown in spring.

Rhapsis exelsa
Japanese Peace Palm/
Bamboo Palm/China Cane/Ground Rattan Cane/Little Lady Palm/Partridge Cane

Family: *Arecaceae*

Use: Ornamental palm for indoors, a greenhouse, or a sunroom, or outdoors from spring to fall.

Origin: South China.

Plant description: Small palm with many thin, bamboo-like canes densely matted with coarse fiber. The leathery, shiny green leaves are divided into up to ten broad segments.

Light and position: Prefers light, but keep away from strong direct sunlight in summer.

Temperature range: Warm to cool, tolerating temperatures down to 41°F (5°C).

Water: Water regularly, allowing the soil to dry out slightly before watering again. This plant will rot and die if overwatered.

Feeding: Feed with a low-nitrogen fertilizer every two weeks from spring to fall. Do not feed during the remainder of the year.

Special care: Avoid direct sun which may cause the leaves to yellow. Repot every second year in early spring.

Pests and diseases: Mealy bugs, scale insects, spider mites, and white fly.

Other species/cultivars: *R. humilis* has thinner stems and palmate leaves divided into up to twenty narrower segments.

Propagation: Sow seeds or remove offsets in early spring.

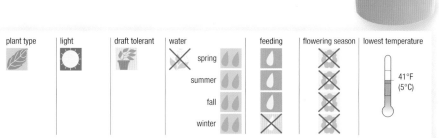

plant type	light	draft tolerant	water		feeding	flowering season	lowest temperature
			spring				
			summer				41°F (5°C)
			fall				
			winter				

Rhododendron simsii
Indian Azalea

Family: *Ericaceae*

Use: Flowering shrub for indoors, a greenhouse or sunroom, or outdoors in summer.

Origin: China and Taiwan.

Plant description: Compact shrub with leathery, ovate leaves and a mass of showy flowers that may entirely cover the plant. The large, semi-double or double flowers are found in a broad range of colors, such as white, salmon, pink, red, crimson, or purple.

Light and position: Shade to filtered sunlight. Keep the plant away from full sun.

Temperature range: Warm to cool, tolerating temperatures down to 41°F (5°C). Prefers a cool position in fall.

Water: Water regularly, allowing the soil to dry out before watering again. The plant prefers soft water. Water more sparingly when it is kept cool.

Feeding: Feed with an acid fertilizer once a month from flowering to fall. Do not feed during the remainder of the year.

Special care: Buy a plant with many flower buds but only a few open flowers to ensure a longer life. Repot after flowering in an acidic, well-drained soil, although it is difficult to make this azalea flower again. Keep it in a warm position, at about 64°F (18°C), to promote flower formation between May and June. From June to August, plant it in a shady spot in the garden. In September, place it in a light, cool position indoors, at about 41–50°F (5–10°C). If placed at a higher temperature one to two months later, the plant may flower again.

Pests and diseases: Aphids, scale insects, spider mites, white fly, and gray mold.

Other species/cultivars: There are innumerable cultivars, varying in plant size and flower color and shape.

Propagation: Stem cuttings can be taken from softwood from late spring to summer.

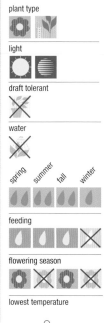

plant type

light

draft tolerant

water

spring summer fall winter

feeding

flowering season

lowest temperature

41°F
(5°C)

Rosa

Potted Rose/Miniature Rose
(hybrids—miniature hybrids)

Family: *Rosaceae*

Use: Flowering shrub for indoors, a greenhouse or sunroom, or outdoors.

Plant description: Small, compact rose with glossy dark green leaves and flowers that may be few or many and are sometimes slightly scented. The flowers have a varying number of petals, making them simple or double, and are found in a broad range of colors, except for blue.

Light and position: Prefers full sunlight; tolerates filtered sun.

Temperature range: Warm to cool. The flowers will last longer if kept in a cool position. This plant is frost-hardy in the garden.

Water: Keep the soil constantly moist and water plentifully from underneath, by standing the pot in water for ten minutes. This plant does not tolerate drying out.

Feeding: Feed with a low-nitrogen fertilizer every two weeks from spring to fall. Do not feed during the remainder of the year.

Special care: Buy a rose that already has a few open flowers to be sure that the rest of the buds will also open. Old flowers can be cut off to make room for new ones. Cutting back the whole plant when the flowers have withered away will make it flower again, if there is sufficient light. Discard after flowering or plant out in the garden.

Pests and diseases: Aphids, spider mites, gray mold, and mildew.

Other species/cultivars: There are innumerable cultivars, varying mainly in plant size and flower color and shape.

Propagation: Stem cuttings can be taken from spring to fall.

plant type

light

draft tolerant

water

spring   summer   fall   winter

feeding

flowering season

lowest temperature

32°F
(0°C)

Saintpaulia ionantha
African Violet/
Usambara Violet

Family: *Gesneriaceae*

Use: Flowering ornamental for indoors, or a greenhouse or sunroom in summer.

Origin: Tanzania.

Plant description: Small perennial forming a rosette of hairy, fleshy, ovate leaves, dark green in color. The single or double flowers may be white, pink, violet-blue, or purple with yellow stamens.

Light and position: Shade to filtered sunlight. Keep the plant away from full sun as this will cause the leaves to yellow.

Temperature range: Prefers a warm position but tolerates temperatures down to 50°F (10°C).

Water: Water regularly from underneath, standing the pot in water for ten minutes, and allow the soil to dry out slightly before watering again. Keep the soil drier during winter if the plant is kept cool.

Feeding: Feed with a low-nitrogen fertilizer once a month from spring to fall. Do not feed during the remainder of the year.

Special care: Repot in well-drained soil every second year in early spring.

Pests and diseases: Aphids, spider mites, gray mold, and mildew.

Other species/cultivars: There are innumerable cultivars, mainly varying in plant size and flower color.

Propagation: By plant division in early spring, or take leaf cuttings when the plant is in growth.

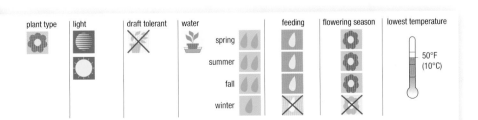

plant type	light	draft tolerant	water		feeding	flowering season	lowest temperature
				spring			
				summer			50°F (10°C)
				fall			
				winter			

Sansevieria trifasciata

Mother-in-Law's Tongue/Snake Plant

Family: *Dracaenaceae*

Use: Sculptural foliage succulent for indoors, a greenhouse, or a sunroom.

Origin: West Africa.

Plant description: Tough succulent with fleshy rootstocks and leathery, upright, lance-shaped leaves, which are variously variegated with gray-green crossbands and yellow margins. The greenish, scented flowers are clustered in loose racemes.

Light and position: Prefers filtered sunlight. Tolerates full sun, but this may cause the leaves to yellow.

Temperature range: Warm to cool, tolerating temperatures down to 41°F (5°C). Prefers a cool position during winter.

Water: Water from underneath, by standing the pot in water for ten minutes. Water sparingly in growing season, allowing the soil to dry out before watering again. Keep the soil almost dry during the rest of the year. This plant tolerates drying out for a few weeks, but will rot and die if overwatered.

Feeding: Feed with a low-nitrogen fertilizer once a month from spring to fall. Do not feed during the remainder of the year.

Special care: The colors of the leaves will fade if the plant is kept in too dark a position. It prefers to be kept cool during winter, at about 50–59°F (10–15°C). Repot every second or third year in spring.

Pests and diseases: Mealy bugs, scale insects, and spider mites.

Other species/cultivars: The cultivar 'Hahnii' forms a low, vase-like rosette of elliptic leaves, which are dark green with pale green crossbands.

Propagation: Divide the plant in spring or take leaf cuttings at any time of year.

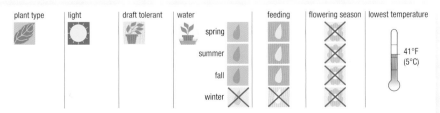

plant type	light	draft tolerant	water		feeding	flowering season	lowest temperature
			spring				
			summer				41°F (5°C)
			fall				
			winter				

Saxifraga stolonifera
Mother of Thousands/
Strawberry Geranium/Saxifrage

Family: *Saxifragaceae*

Use: Foliage ornamental for indoors, a greenhouse or sunroom, or outdoors in summer. Ideal for a hanging basket or as groundcover.

Origin: China and Japan.

Plant description: Compact perennial that forms a rosette of heart-shaped, hairy, dark green leaves and bears many small, white to pink flowers clustered in erect panicles. The leaves are colored dark green with silver-gray patches along the veins and purple undersides. Many rooting plantlets are produced on hanging, threadlike stems.

Light and position: Shade or filtered sunlight. Keep the plant away from full sun.

Temperature range: Warm to cool, tolerating temperatures down to 41°F (5°C). Prefers a cool position during winter.

Water: Keep the soil constantly moist all year. Avoid drying out.

Feeding: Feed with a low-nitrogen fertilizer every two weeks from spring to fall. Do not feed during the remainder of the year.

Special care: This plant is fast-growing and easy to maintain. It prefers to be kept cool during winter, at about 50–59°F (10–15°C). Repot every year in early spring.

Pests and diseases: Aphids, mealy bugs, and gray mold.

Other species/cultivars: 'Tricolor' is a smaller cultivar with dark green leaves variegated with ivory white, pink, or rosy crimson.

Propagation: Repot rooting plantlets at any time of year.

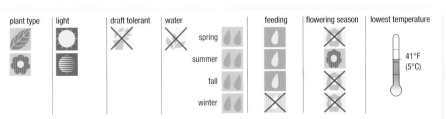

plant type	light	draft tolerant	water		feeding	flowering season	lowest temperature
				spring			
				summer			41°F (5°C)
				fall			
				winter			

Schefflera arboricola
Heptapleurum/Parasol Plant
Family: *Araliaceae*

Use: Ornamental foliage plant for indoors, or a greenhouse or sunroom in summer.

Origin: Taiwan.

Plant description: Epiphytic shrub with long-stalked, palmate leaves, each comprising seven to eleven leathery leaflets.

Light and position: Prefers filtered sun, but tolerates direct sunlight.

Temperature range: Warm to cool, tolerating temperatures down to 41°F (5°C).

Water: Water regularly, allowing the soil to dry out before watering again. This plant will not tolerate overwatering.

Feeding: Feed with a low-nitrogen fertilizer every two weeks from spring to fall. Do not feed during the remainder of the year.

Special care: Because this plant needs support, it can be trained to a moss-covered pole. Repot every second or third year in early spring, cutting back at the same time to promote a more compact growth.

Pests and diseases: Aphids, mealy bugs, scale insects, spider mites, and gray mold.

Other species/cultivars: Several cultivars with varying leaf size are available, some with yellow-variegated foliage.

Propagation: Cuttings from semi-ripe shoots can be taken all year round.

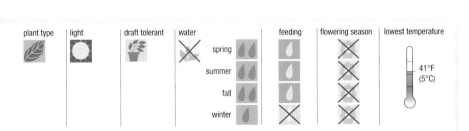

plant type	light	draft tolerant	water		feeding	flowering season	lowest temperature
			spring				41°F (5°C)
			summer				
			fall				
			winter				

Schlumbergera x *buckleyi*
Holiday Cactus/
Christmas Cactus
Family: *Cactaceae*

Use: Winter-flowering succulent for indoors, or a greenhouse or sunroom in summer.

Plant description: Epiphytic succulent with drooping chains of flat, leaf-like stems, toothed at the margins. The pendant flowers are found at the end of the stems in a broad range of bright colors, such as white, salmon, pink, or red.

Light and position: Filtered sunlight. Keep the plant away from full sun from spring to fall.

Temperature range: Warm to cool, tolerating temperatures down to 59°F (15°C).

Water: This plant will rot and die if overwatered. Water regularly during flowering, allowing the soil to dry out before watering again. Keep the soil drier during winter if the plant is kept cool.

Feeding: Feed every two weeks with a weak fertilizer during flowering and active growth. Do not feed during the remainder of the year.

Special care: This succulent will flower during short-day conditions in fall (less than twelve hours of light per day is required for at least a month). Repot every second year in early spring, using well-drained, peaty soil. At the same time the plant can be cut back to promote a more compact growth.

Pests and diseases: Mealy bugs, scale insects, and spider mites.

Other species/cultivars: There are many cultivars, offering a range of flower colors.

Propagation: Flat stem cuttings, two to three segments long, can be taken in spring and summer.

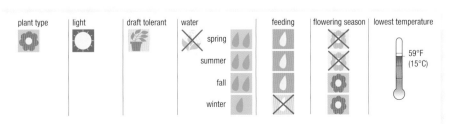

Scindapsus pictus
Satin Pothos/Silver Pothos/
Satin Potho

Family: *Araceae*

Use: Foliage climber for indoors, a greenhouse or sunroom, or outdoors. Ideal for a trellis, hanging basket, or hoop.
Origin: Malay Peninsula.
Plant description:
Creeping climber with waxy, ovate to heart-shaped leaves, colored gray-green with silver blotches.
Light and position: Tolerates a broad spectrum of light, but should be kept away from full sun.
Temperature range: Warm to cool, tolerating temperatures down to 59°F (15°C).
Water: Water regularly all year round, allowing the soil to dry out slightly before watering again. Mist the plant every week or so with a hand-spray to maintain humidity.
Feeding: Feed with a weak fertilizer every two weeks from spring to fall. Do not feed during the remainder of the year.
Special care: This plant prefers high humidity. It requires support and so is ideal for placing in a hanging basket, tying to a trellis, or training to a hoop.

The climber should be repotted every second or third year in spring. At the same time it can be cut back to promote more compact growth.
Pests and diseases: Mealy bugs, scale insects, spider mites, and gray mold.
Other species/cultivars: 'Argyraeus' has silver-blotched, bluish-green leaves with silver margins.
Propagation: Stem cuttings can be taken at any time of year.

plant type	light	draft tolerant	water		feeding	flowering season	lowest temperature
			spring				
			summer				59°F (15°C)
			fall				
			winter				

Sedum burrito

Burro's Tail/Donkey's Tail

Family: *Crassulaceae*

Use: Sculptural succulent for indoors, a greenhouse or sunroom, or outdoors in summer.

Origin: Mexico.

Plant description: Hanging succulent with stems closely covered by fleshy, cocoon-shaped, gray-green leaves. Small flowers in red to pink grow at the tip of the stems.

Light and position: Prefers full sunlight, but tolerates filtered sun.

Temperature range: Warm to cool, preferring a cool position during winter. Tolerates temperatures down to 41°F (5°C).

Water: Water regularly from spring to fall, allowing the soil to dry out before watering again. Keep the soil almost dry for the rest of the year, especially if the plant is kept cool. It will tolerate drying out for a month in cool conditions but will rot and die if overwatered.

Feeding: Feed with a weak fertilizer every two weeks from spring to fall. Do not feed during the remainder of the year.

Special care: Protect the plant against rain if it is placed outdoors. It prefers a dormant period during winter, when it should be kept in a light, cool position at about 50–59°F (10–15°C). Repot every second or third year in early spring, in well-drained soil.

Pests and diseases: Gray mold.

Other species/cultivars: *S. morganianum* has longer, spindle-shaped leaves. *S. sieboldii* has round, glaucous-blue leaves in whorls of three.

Propagation: By plant division, stem cuttings, or single leaves taken from spring to summer.

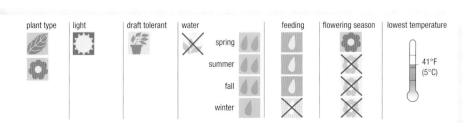

plant type	light	draft tolerant	water		feeding	flowering season	lowest temperature
				spring			
				summer			41°F (5°C)
				fall			
				winter			

Senecio herreianus
String of Beads
Family: *Asteraceae*

Use: Sculptural succulent for indoors, a greenhouse, or a sunroom. Ideal for a hanging basket, trellis, or hoop.
Origin: Namibia.
Plant description: Fast-growing succulent with fine, trailing stems studded with round, fleshy leaves, bluish in color. In fall, cup-shaped heads of tiny, white flowers are produced near the tip of the stems.
Light and position: Prefers filtered sun. Tolerates full sunlight, but this might result in yellow leaves.
Temperature range: Warm to cool, tolerating temperatures down to 32°F (0°C). Prefers a cool position during winter.
Water: Water regularly during growing season, allowing the soil to dry out before watering again. Keep the soil almost dry for the rest of the year. The plant will tolerate drying out for a month in cool conditions.
Feeding: Feed with a low-nitrogen fertilizer once a month from spring to fall. Do not feed during the remainder of the year.
Special care: This plant needs support and so is suitable for placing in a hanging basket, tying to a trellis, or training to a hoop. It prefers a dormant period during winter, when it should be kept in a light, cool position, at about 50–59°F (10–15°C). Repot every second year in early spring.
Pests and diseases: Aphids, mildew, and gray mold.
Other species/cultivars: *S. citriformis* has lemon-shaped leaves.
Propagation: Divide the plant or take stem cuttings from spring to summer.

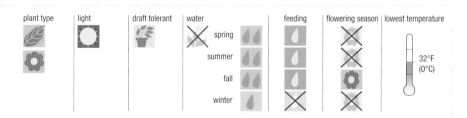

plant type	light	draft tolerant	water		feeding	flowering season	lowest temperature
			spring				
			summer				32°F (0°C)
			fall				
			winter				

Sinningia
Brazilian Gloxinia/
Florist's Gloxinia (hybrids)

Family: *Gesneriaceae*

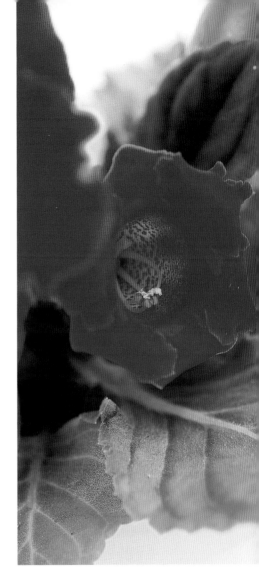

Use: Flowering plant for indoors, or a greenhouse or sunroom in summer.

Origin: Brazil.

Plant description: Tuberous, nearly stemless herb with large, white, velvety leaves with round-toothed margins. The large, upright, bell-shaped flowers, which may be single or double, come in a broad range of colors, from white to dark red or purple.

Light and position: Filtered sunlight. Keep away from full sun.

Temperature range: Warm, but cooler during winter. When dormant, the plant tolerates temperatures down to 32°F (0°C).

Water: Water from underneath, by standing the pot in water for ten minutes. Keep the soil constantly moist and avoid drying out.

Feeding: Feed with a low-nitrogen fertilizer every two weeks from spring to summer. Do not feed during the remainder of the year.

Special care: This plant needs a dormant period during winter. Stop watering in fall, when the plant starts to wither. Remove the withered parts of the plant and keep the tubers dry and frost-free, at 41–50°F (5–10°C). In early spring, repot the tubers, place them in a warmer position, and start watering again.

Pests and diseases: Aphids and gray mold.

Other species/cultivars: Many cultivars varying in flower color are available.

Propagation: From tubers or leaf cuttings in spring.

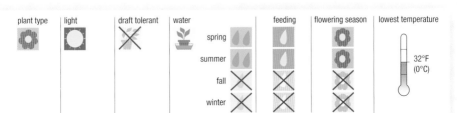

plant type	light	draft tolerant	water		feeding	flowering season	lowest temperature
			spring	💧💧	💧	🌸	
			summer	💧💧	💧	🌸	32°F (0°C)
			fall	✕	✕	✕	
			winter	✕	✕	✕	

Solanum pseudocapsicum

Jerusalem Cherry/Winter Cherry/
Madeira Winter Cherry

Family: *Solanaceae*

Use: Fruit-bearing ornamental shrub for indoors, a greenhouse or sunroom, or outdoors from spring to fall.
Origin: Madeira.
Plant description: Compact, branching shrub with dark green, lance-shaped leaves. The small, star-like, white flowers are followed by globular fruits, colored first green, later scarlet-orange.
Light and position: Prefers full sunlight, but tolerates filtered sun.
Temperature range: Warm to cool, preferring a cool position in winter. Tolerates temperatures down to 32°F (0°C). The fruit will last longer if the plant is kept cool.
Water: The plant tolerates drying out but will die if overwatered. Water regularly from spring to fall, allowing the soil to dry out before watering again. Keep the soil even drier if the plant is kept cool in winter.
Feeding: Feed with a low-nitrogen fertilizer every two weeks during flowering until the fruit are formed, and afterward only once a month until fall. Do not feed during the remainder of the year.
Special care: Keep the plant away from children, as its fruit is poisonous. It prefers a dormant period during winter, when it should be kept in a light, cool position at about 41–50°F (5–10°C). Repot every year in spring; long shoots can be cut back at the same time. The plant will flower again in spring.
Pests and diseases: Aphids, mealy bugs, spider mites, and gray mold.
Other species/cultivars: Different cultivars offer a variety of fruit sizes and colors.
Propagation: Softwood cuttings can be taken from spring to summer.

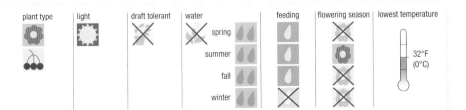

Soleirolia soleirolii
Angel's Tears/Baby's Tears
Family: *Urticaceae*

Use: Sculptural, foliage ornamental for indoors, a greenhouse or sunroom, or outdoors from spring to fall. Can be used as groundcover.
Origin: Europe.
Plant description: Low, creeping herb forming dense mats of foliage. The thread-like branches bear small, round, grass-green leaves and insignificant, green flowers, which form in the leaf-axils.
Light and position: Filtered sunlight. Keep the plant away from full sun.
Temperature range: Prefers a cool position, tolerating temperatures down to 32°F (0°C). A cool position during winter will promote flower formation.
Water: Water regularly, standing the pot in water for ten minutes. Avoid getting water on the leaves and stems, as this makes the plant vulnerable to fungus disease. Allow the soil to dry out slightly before watering again, and keep it drier during winter if the plant is kept cool. Mist frequently with a hand-spray to maintain high humidity.
Feeding: Feed regularly with a weak fertilizer in summer. Do not feed during the remainder of the year.
Special care: This plant enjoys high humidity. It prefers a dormant period during winter, when it should be kept well lit and cool, at about 41–50°F (5–10°C). The plant can be cut back in spring to promote new growth if it is in a light position. Repot every year in spring.
Pests and diseases: Aphids, mealy bugs, and gray mold.
Other species/cultivars: Cultivars with yellow or gray-green leaves are grown.
Propagation: By plant division in late spring.

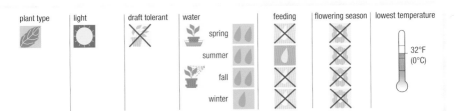

plant type | light | draft tolerant | water | feeding | flowering season | lowest temperature

spring / summer / fall / winter

32°F (0°C)

plant type

light

draft tolerant

water

spring *summer* *fall* *winter*

feeding

flowering season

lowest temperature

59°F
(15°C)

Spathiphyllum wallisii
Peace Lily

Family: *Araceae*

Use: Flowering perennial for indoors.
Origin: Costa Rica, Panama, Colombia, and Venezuela.
Plant description: Herbaceous plant with shiny, dark green, lance-shaped to oblong leaves and showy, white spathes, each one cupping a yellow spadix.
Light and position: Tolerates shade to filtered sun. Keep the plant away from direct sunlight.
Temperature range: Warm, preferring temperatures around 64°F (18°C). Tolerates temperatures down to 59°F (15°C).
Water: Water plentifully from spring to fall, more sparingly during the rest of the year. Tolerates standing in water, but not drying out. Mist the plant frequently with a hand-spray to maintain high humidity.
Feeding: Feed with a weak fertilizer every two weeks from spring to fall. Do not feed during the remainder of the year as this may scorch the leaves and cause the flowers to die prematurely.
Special care: Prefers high humidity. Old flower stems can be cut off at any time of year to allow room for new flowering, and the plant should be repotted every year in spring.
Pests and diseases: Spider mites and gray mold.
Other species/cultivars: There are many cultivars, with varying sizes of plant and flower.
Propagation: By plant division in spring.

Stephanotis floribunda
Madagascar Jasmine/
Bridal Wreath/Wax Flower/
Chaplet Flower/Floradora

Family: *Asclepiadaceae*

Use: Flowering climber for indoors, a greenhouse, or a sunroom. Needs support: ideal for small trellis.

Origin: Madagascar.

Plant description: Liana with leathery, elliptic leaves, growing in opposite pairs on the stem, and waxy, white flowers, which are tubular in shape and fragrant.

Light and position: Filtered sunlight. Keep the plant away from full sun from spring to fall as this may scorch the leaves.

Temperature range: Warm to cool, preferring a cool position during winter. Tolerates temperatures down to 59°F (15°C).

Water: Keep the soil constantly moist when the plant is flowering, as drying out will cause the flower buds to drop. The soil should be drier during winter if the plant is kept cool.

Feeding: Feed with a low-nitrogen fertilizer every two weeks from spring to fall. Do not feed during the remainder of the year.

Special care: Buy a plant with at least one open flower to be sure that the other flowers will open as well. The plant should be kept away from drafts during flowering. From fall to early spring, place it in a light, cool position, at 59–68°F (15–20°C), to promote the formation of flower buds. Repot every second or third year in early spring; long shoots can be cut back at the same time.

Pests and diseases: Aphids, mealy bugs, scale insects, spider mites, and gray mold.

Other species/cultivars: None.

Propagation: Stem cuttings from softwood or semi-ripe nodal cuttings can be taken at any time of year. Place the cuttings in a heated propagator or on a propagation blanket, with a bottom heat of 68–77°F (20–25°C).

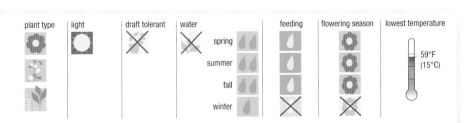

plant type	light	draft tolerant	water		feeding	flowering season	lowest temperature
				spring			
				summer			59°F (15°C)
				fall			
				winter			

Streptocarpus
Twisted Stalk/
Cape Primrose (hybrids)

Family: *Gesneriaceae*

Use: A flowering plant for indoors, a greenhouse or sunroom, or outdoors in summer.

Plant description: Compact, herbaceous perennial with large, broadly oblong leaves and stalked inflorescences with a mass of nodding, tubular flowers.

Light and position: Filtered sunlight; keep away from full sun.

Temperature range: Warm to cool, tolerating temperatures down to 41°F (5°C).

Water: Keep the soil constantly moist from spring to fall, watering from underneath by standing the pot in water for ten minutes. Water more sparingly if the plant is kept cool during winter. Avoid letting cold water come into contact with the leaves.

Feeding: Feed with a weak fertilizer every two weeks from spring to fall. Do not feed during the remainder of the year.

Special care: Repot the plant in a well-drained compost every year in early spring.

Pests and diseases: Aphids, mealy bugs, and spider mites.

Other species/cultivars: Many cultivars are available with a wide range of flower colors, from white to pink, red, purple, and blue.

Propagation: Take stem-tip or leaf cuttings from spring to fall. Plants can be divided in spring.

plant type	light	draft tolerant	water		feeding	flowering season	lowest temperature
			spring				
			summer				41°F (5°C)
			fall				
			winter				

Syngonium podophyllum
Arrowhead Vine/
Goosefoot Plant

Family: *Araceae*

Use: Tough foliage climber for indoors, a greenhouse, or a sunroom. Ideal for a trellis, hoop, or hanging basket.

Origin: Mexico, Guatemala, El Salvador, and Costa Rica.

Plant description: Compact climber with large, stalked, arrow-shaped leaves in shades of yellow-green.

Light and position: Tolerates a shady to filtered-sun position. Keep the plant away from direct sunlight.

Temperature range: Warm to cool, tolerating temperatures down to 59°F (15°C).

Water: Keep the soil constantly moist. Drying out or overwatering will cause the leaves to yellow. Mist the plant frequently with a hand-spray to maintain high humidity.

Feeding: Feed with a low-nitrogen fertilizer every two weeks from spring to fall. Do not feed during the remainder of the year.

Special care: This plant needs support, such as a small trellis, hoop, or hanging basket, and prefers high humidity. It should be repotted every second or third year in spring. At the same time, the plant can be cut back to promote a more compact growth.

Pests and diseases: Aphids, scale insects, and spider mites.

Other species/cultivars: The cultivar 'Arrow' has large, green leaves with white ornamentation following the mid and lateral veins. 'Pixie' has grass-green leaves with yellow-green ornamentation. 'White Butterfly' has yellow-green leaves with dark green ornamentation.

Propagation: Cuttings of leaf buds or softwood stem tips can be taken in summer.

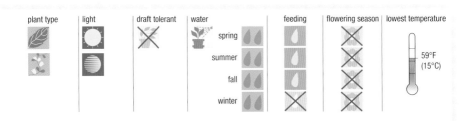

plant type	light	draft tolerant	water		feeding	flowering season	lowest temperature
				spring			
				summer			59°F (15°C)
				fall			
				winter			

Tillandsia cyanea
Pink Quill/Air Plant

Family: *Bromeliaceae*

Use: Tough, flowering bromeliad for indoors, a greenhouse or sunroom, or outdoors in summer.

Origin: Ecuador.

Plant description: Perennial epiphyte bearing a rosette of linear, dark green leaves and a showy, short spike of flat, vivid pink bracts and violet flowers.

Light and position: Tolerates a broad spectrum of light, but should be kept away from direct sunlight.

Temperature range: Warm to cool, tolerating temperatures down to 41°F (5°C).

Water: Water with lukewarm water inside the rosette. The plant tolerates drying out for a few weeks, but mist the plant frequently with a hand-spray to maintain high humidity.

Feeding: Feed inside the rosette with a weak fertilizer once a month from spring to fall. Do not feed during the remainder of the year.

Special care: Prefers high humidity. The rosette should always contain water except when the plant is kept at low temperatures. Repot the offsets in spring.

Pests and diseases: Mealy bugs, scale insects, and spider mites.

Other species/cultivars: 'Anita' has broader leaves and more brightly colored bracts and flowers.
C. flabellata bears a branching inflorescence with shiny red bracts in narrow spikes.

Propagation: Divide the offsets from the parent plant in spring.

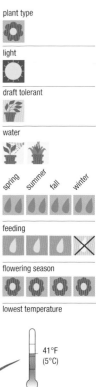

plant type

light

draft tolerant

water

spring summer fall winter

feeding

flowering season

lowest temperature

41°F
(5°C)

Tradescantia fluminensis

Wandering Sailor/
Wandering Jew

Family: *Commelinaceae*

Use: Foliage creeper for indoors, or a greenhouse or sunroom in summer. Can be used as groundcover. Some cultivars are ideal for hanging baskets.

Origin: Southeast Brazil and Argentina.

Plant description: Free-growing creeper with soft stems and shiny, ovate leaves, which are often striped or banded and found in a broad range of colors. Rooting takes place at the nodes.

Light and position: Filtered sunlight. Keep the plant away from full sun.

Temperature range: Warm to cool, tolerating temperatures down to 41°F (5°C).

Water: Water regularly all year round, allowing the soil to dry out slightly before watering again.

Feeding: Feed with a low-nitrogen fertilizer every two weeks from spring to fall. Do not feed during the remainder of the year.

Special care: This plant is very easy to grow. It can be cut back in early spring to promote a more compact growth. Repot every second year in spring.

Pests and diseases: Aphids, spider mites, white fly, and gray mold.

Other species/cultivars: There are many different species and cultivars. *Gibasis geniculata* forms long stems bearing small, shiny olive-green leaves with purplish undersides and many small, white flowers. *T. spathacea* has a rosette of stiff, striped leaves and small, white flowers surrounded by boat-shaped bracts.

Propagation: Take stem cuttings at any time of year or divide the plant in spring.

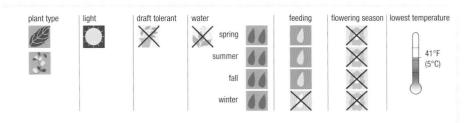

plant type	light	draft tolerant	water		feeding	flowering season	lowest temperature
			spring				
			summer				41°F (5°C)
			fall				
			winter				

plant type

light

draft tolerant

water

spring   summer   fall   winter

feeding

flowering season

lowest temperature

41°F
(5°C)

Vriesea splendens
Flaming Sword

Family: *Bromeliaceae*

Use: Tough, flowering bromeliad for indoors, a greenhouse or sunroom, or outdoors in summer.

Origin: Venezuela and Surinam.

Plant description: Stemless bromeliad with a rosette of leathery, dark green leaves marked with purple crossbands. The long flower spike is sword-shaped, with vivid orange-scarlet bracts and yellow flowers.

Light and position: Tolerates a broad spectrum of light, but should be kept away from direct sun.

Temperature range: Warm to cool, tolerating temperatures down to 41°F (5°C).

Water: Water with lukewarm water inside the rosette. The plant tolerates drying out for a few weeks. Mist the plant frequently with a hand-spray to maintain high humidity.

Feeding: Feed regularly with a weak fertilizer inside the rosette from spring to fall. Do not feed during the remainder of the year.

Special care: This plant prefers high humidity. The rosette should always contain water except when the plant is kept at low temperatures. Repot the offsets in spring.

Pests and diseases: Mealy bugs, scale insects, and spider mites.

Other species/cultivars: There are many other species and cultivars. 'Annie' has glossy dark green leaves and yellow and red bracts. 'Christiana' has broader leaves and a wide flower spike of glossy red bracts. 'Fire' bears a flaming orange, sword-shaped flower spike.

Propagation: Offsets can be separated from the plant in spring.

Yucca elephantipes
Elephant Yucca

Family: *Agavaceae*

Use: Tough, sculptural, foliage plant for indoors, a greenhouse or sunroom, or outdoors in summer.

Origin: Mexico and Guatemala.

Plant description: Small, trunk-forming tree with rosettes of broad, dark green leaves, which have a leathery texture, rough margins, and a soft apex.

Light and position: Prefers full sunlight; tolerates filtered sun.

Temperature range: Warm to cool, preferring a cool position during winter. Tolerates temperatures down to 32°F (0°C).

Water: Water regularly, allowing the soil to dry out before watering again. Water more sparingly if the plant is kept cool during winter.

Feeding: Feed with a weak fertilizer every two weeks from spring to fall. Do not feed during the remainder of the year.

Special care: The plant, including its woody trunk, can be cut back in early spring. It prefers a dormant period during winter, when it should be kept in a light, cool position at about 50–59°F (10–15°C). Repot every second or third year in early spring.

Pests and diseases: Aphids, mealy bugs, scale insects, and spider mites.

Other species/cultivars: The cultivar 'Puck' has light green leaves bordered with white.

Propagation: Plant division can take place in late winter and early spring. Take softwood cuttings from spring to summer and bud cuttings in spring.

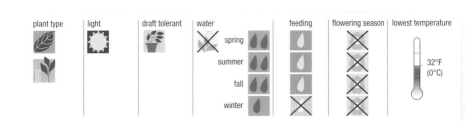

plant type	light	draft tolerant	water		feeding	flowering season	lowest temperature
				spring			
				summer			32°F (0°C)
				fall			
				winter			

Zamioculcas zamiifolia
Arum Fern/Aroid Palm

Family: *Araceae*

Use: Tough, sculptural, foliage plant for indoors, or a greenhouse or sunroom in summer.

Origin: Tropical East Africa.

Plant description: Upright, slow-growing succulent that forms underground bulbs. The large, pinnate leaves are shiny dark green with swollen stalks.

Light and position: Tolerates a broad spectrum of light from direct sun to shade.

Temperature range: Warm, cooler during winter. Tolerates temperatures down to 60°F (15°C).

Water: Water regularly during growing season, allowing the soil to dry out slightly before watering again. The plant tolerates drying out, but not overwatering, which will cause the leaves to yellow or drop. Water more sparingly if the plant is kept cool during winter.

Feeding: Feed with a low-nitrogen fertilizer once a month from spring to fall. Do not feed during the remainder of the year.

Special care: Repot every second or third year in early spring.

Pests and diseases: Aphids and spider mites.

Other species/cultivars: None.

Propagation: New plants can be produced from small leaflets cut from the leaves in early spring. Repot the leaflets, which will develop bulbs and later young plants.

plant type

light

draft tolerant

water

spring · summer · fall · winter

feeding

flowering season

lowest temperature

60°F
(15°C)

Zantedeschia
Calla/Calla Lily/Arum Lily (hybrids)
Family: *Araceae*

Use: Flowering ornamental for indoors, a greenhouse or sunroom, or outdoors from spring to fall.

Plant description: Tuberous, perennial herb with elegant flowers and attractive foliage. Stout stalks bear showy, trumpet-shaped spathe in bright colors from pure white to yellow, peach, salmon, red, or purple. The large, arrow- to lance-shaped leaves range in color from yellow-green to dark green, and sometimes show white spotting.

Light and position: Tolerates a broad spectrum of light, from shady to sunny positions.

Temperature range: Warm to cool, tolerating temperatures down to 41°F (5°C). The flowers will last longer, and their color will be brighter, if the plant is placed in a cool position.

Water: Water regularly, allowing the soil to dry out slightly before watering again. This plant will rot and die if overwatered.

Feeding: None.

Special care: The plant will wither in fall. Discard after flowering, as it is difficult to make it flower again.

Pests and diseases: Aphids and spider mites.

Other species/cultivars: There are many hybrids with varying colors of spathe. *Z. aethiopica* has pure white spathe and dark green, heart-shaped leaves.

Propagation: By division of rhizomes in spring or from seeds sown in spring.

plant type	light	draft tolerant	water		feeding	flowering season	lowest temperature
			spring				
			summer				41°F (5°C)
			fall				
			winter				

Glossary

Aerial root A root which grows up above the level of the soil, often seen in philodendrons and *Monstera deliciosa*, which can extract moisture from the air.

Annual A plant which completes its whole life-cycle within one year of being grown from seed.

Anther The male part of a flower usually consisting of two lobes or 'sacs' which contain the pollen grains. See *stamen*.

Apex The tip of the plant stem.

Bract A modified leaf, shaped like a leaf or flower petal. Bracts are often highly colored, as in the *Poinsettia*, and may support a less showy flower.

Bromeliad A member of the *Bromeliaceae*, or pineapple family. Bromeliads are epiphytic plants and can be grown supported on tree bark rather than in soil.

Bulb A fleshy bud growing underground which stores food and protects new growth within its overlapping layers.

Calyx The whorl of sepals which protects the flower while in the bud stage.

Corolla The petals of a flower which may be separate or fused to form a funnel, trumpet, or bell.

Corona An outgrowth of petal tissue in the center of flowers such as narcissus and daffodils.

Creeper A plant with trailing growth which puts down roots at intervals along its growth.

Cultivar A term for a plant which has been grown in cultivation, rather than originating in the wild.

Cyme A compound inflorescence made up of repeated lateral branching. In the monochasial cyme, each branch ends in a flower bud and one lateral branch. In the dichasial cyme, each branch ends in a flower bud and two opposite branches.

Deciduous A term describing plants which shed their leaves when inactive, usually during winter.

Division Propagation method in which the rootball of a mature plant is split and the sections potted separately.

Dormant period A temporary period in which a plant ceases to grow at all. This often occurs during the winter months.

Epiphyte A plant which can derive moisture and nutrients from the air or decaying plant matter and therefore does not need to grow in soil, but can support itself when growing in bark or shallow moss.

Foliage plant A plant which is grown indoors to display the beauty of its leaves. Although some bear flowers, these are usually insignificant.

Foliar feed Fertilizer which is sprayed onto the leaves of the plant and can be rapidly absorbed.

Fungus A parasitic form of plant life including microscopic organisms which cause such houseplant diseases as mildew and botrytis.

Genus A term which refers to a group of plants with similar characteristics which can be sub-divided into separate species. Several genera of fundamentally similar plants make up a family.

Herbaceous A term for plants with non-woody stems which last for one growing season only, dying down once flowering and seeding has taken place. Annual and biennial plants die totally, but perennials spring up from the root at the start of each growing season.

Hybrid A plant which is bred by cross-fertilizing two plants of the same family, although not necessarily of the same genus or variety.

Inflorescence A term commonly applied to a cluster of flowers, a flower head, or spike growing on one main stem. Also a general term for the flowering of a plant.

Insectivorous A term for plants which catch insects and other small animals. They are capable of digesting the animal tissue and utilizing the nitrogen and other substances. (Also sometimes called carnivorous).

Lateral Shoots which arise on the sides of the main or leading stems.

Latex A white/clear liquid produced by certain plants when the stem is cut or damaged. May irritate the skin.

Leaf-axil The angle between a leaf or leaf stalk and the stem on which it is carried. A growth from the axil is called an axillary bud.

Liana Tropical plant with a long, woody, climbing stem.

Lobe A section of a leaf, bract, etc., which is partially separated from the main part of the organ like a cape or isthmus. It is used also for the petal-like divisions at the mouth of a tubular flower.

Margin The edge of a section of a plant, usually the leaf.

Node The part of the stem where a leaf is joined and a lateral shoot grows out.

Offset A small, new plant which grows naturally from its parent; it can be detached and propagated separately.

Panicle An inflorescence made up of several racemes or cymes.

Pendant Describes plant parts that hang down.

Perennial A term applied to a plant which lives indefinitely. In houseplants, this means surviving through at least three seasons of growth, and often much more.

Perianth The two outer whorls (calyx and corolla or sepals and petals) which first protect and then display the generative parts. In general, perianth is used when the petals and sepals look alike, as in a tulip.

Petiole A stem or stalk which carries a leaf.

Pinnate The term for a compound leaf in which the leaflets are carried in pairs on opposite sides of the stem. In plants where there is a further division of each part of the compound leaf, the arrangement is called bipinnate.

Plantlet A small plant produced on the runners or stems of a parent plant.

Propagation Technique of forming a new plant by means of cuttings or divisions of a mature plant.

Pruning Cutting back the growth of a plant selectively to encourage bushiness, a compact shape, and better flowering.

Pseudobulbs A swollen aerial stem typical of epiphytic orchids.

Raceme An inflorescence composed of a central or main stem bearing stalked blooms at intervals.

Rhizome A thick, horizontal stem, usually growing underground, from which buds and roots are grown.

Rootball The mixture of roots and potting mix visible when a plant is lifted from its pot.

Rootstock The main stem of the plant with its roots.

Rosette The name given to an arrangement of clustered leaves radiating from a central area, either carried on a single stem or on separate stems.

Sepal The outer whorl of the perianth of a flower, usually green but sometimes colored and petal-like.

Shrub A plant with branching, woody stems which remains relatively compact in growth, unlike a tree.

Soft water Lime-free water such as rainwater or boiled, cooled water.

Spadix A fleshy spike which carries small flowers embedded in its surface.

Spathe A large bract, often brightly colored, which acts as a protective sheath for a spadix.

Species A sub-division of a genus of plants forming a distinct grouping of plants which can fertilize each other and grow from seed without being specially cultivated.

Sphagnum moss A spongy bog moss, useful in cultivating houseplants because of its high capacity to hold water.

Spike An elongated, unbranched infloresence (flowers growing directly from a central stalk).

Spikelet A unit of inflorescence in grasses.

Spore The reproductive cell of a fern or moss, acting in the same way as a seed from a flowering plant. Ferns usually carry spores in raised cases on the undersides of the fronds.

Stamen The male unit of a flower comprising two anther lobes joined together at the top of a filament (stalk). See *anther*.

Succulent A plant with fleshy stems and leaves which are able to store moisture.

Tendril A fine, twining thread arising from the leaf or stem of a plant which clings to a frame or surface, enabling the plant to climb.

Terrestrial A plant which grows in soil in its natural habitat, as opposed to an epiphytic or an aquatic plant.

Tough A term describing a plant which can withstand prolonged exposure to cold temperatures.

Tuber A swollen stem, usually underground, which stores food and produces new growth.

Umbel An inflorescence of stalked flowers, all of which arise and radiate from the tip of the main stem.

Variegated A term which refers to plants with patterned, spotty, or blotchy leaves.

Variety A member of a plant species which differs from the others by a natural alteration such as in the color of the leaves or flowers. The term is often applied to plants bred in cultivation, which strictly should be called cultivars.

Index

Acknowledgments

Thanks to Flora-Dania for their advice and help in providing the suppliers for this book.

Picture on page 14 © Elizabeth Whiting & Associates/CORBIS.

Thanks to Clifton Nurseries Ltd (www.clifton.co.uk) for its kind support in supplying several of the plants pictured in this book.

All other photographs and illustrations are the copyright of Quarto Publishing plc.

key to symbols

**Fold out this flap to find an at-a-glance key explaining all
the symbols used throughout the book.**

Key to symbols

Plant type

 Foliage plant

 Flowering plant

 Climbing or trailing plant

 Fruiting plant

 Large plant

Light

 Plant prefers full sun

 Plant prefers indirect light

 Plant prefers shade

Draft tolerance

 Tolerates drafts

 Will not tolerate drafts

Watering

 Plant requires misting

Plant requires steeping

Water plant in its urn-like rosette

No special watering requirements

The symbols below are arranged by season

 Water regularly

 Water less frequently

 Do not water

Feeding

 Feed regularly

 Do not feed

Flowering season

 In flower

No flowers

Lowest temperature

 50°F (-10°C) Indicates the lowest temperature at which the plant will survive